Praise for
The Truth About Being a Leader...
And Nothing But the Truth

"If you've ever met Dr. Otazo, you certainly would read her new *Truth* book. She is as she writes—engaging, pithy, memorable. Take 'Truth 33: Questions Unite; Answers Divide.' Now ain't that the truth. And there are 51 other bon mots just like it. Open the book. Read a truth. You will smile, reflect, and be a better leader for it."

**—Paul McLoughlin, The Krow Show with Paul McLoughlin,
aka 'the work_wonk,' Live Online Radio, Wednesdays,
1 pm Eastern, VoiceAmericaBusiness.com**

"This is a sharply written book with smart insights into the business world. Dr. Otazo is blunt, honest, and concise—exactly the advice a real leader needs."

—Rudy Giuliani

"The Truth About Being a Leader is a book that offers practical advice about the very difficult and elusive art of leadership. Dr. Otazo's book offers real lessons for anyone who is tasked to lead people!"
—Marc Morial, CEO, National Urban League

"This book takes you on a tour 'behind closed doors' of the landscape of leadership. Just as great military leaders have to know the ground where a future battle will take place, you as an aspiring leader will need to know about the terrain that is covered in this book. And the scope of the landscape here is impressive. It is not just the expected areas such as vision, communication, and team work, but also the important and often undiscussable matters such as how to select an assistant, the role of BS, and the care and use of your body as a leadership act. You can either hire Dr. Otazo as an executive coach to impart her years of wisdom from working with great leaders—or you can read this compelling book and get the secrets here."

**—Douglas T. (Tim) Hall Professor of Organizational Behavior,
Director, Executive Development Roundtable,
Boston University School of Management**

"The simple truth is that everyone who is, or aspires to be, in a leadership position should keep this book close to hand at all times. An excellent distillation of the essential elements of leadership, this is a practical resource tool that speaks with the voice of a trusted friend and advisor. Clear and concise, this book has something useful to say on just about every facet of leadership. Dr Otazo, in print as in person, is always wise and always pertinent."
—*Rosemarie Wallace, Regional Managing Director, Reader's Digest Asia*

"I very much enjoyed reading *The Truth about Being a Leader*, which accurately reflects so many of the situations I have encountered in 40 years of business life."
—*Maarten van den Bergh, Chairman Lloyds TSB Group plc*

"From her own vast experience as a coach and leader herself, Dr. Otazo has written a book that really does tell the truth about what it takes to be a leader. Those who want a book that will give easy answers about leadership should look elsewhere. The answers given here aren't the easy ones—but they are the correct ones. This is the book that I will be giving to my own clients in leadership positions—and constantly referring to myself!"
—*Mark Forster, Time Management Guru, Author of* **Get Everything Done and Still Have Time to Play** *and other books*

"Put away all those leadership theories and pick up this book. Dr. Otazo presents real issues with pragmatic strategies and immediately actionable tactics. A must-read for experienced and emerging leaders and their coaches."
—*Sheryl Spanier, President, Sheryl Spanier & Company, Leadership coaching guru*

"Whereas academics have leadership theory and successful leaders like Jack Welch (*On Winning*) can relate their experiences, Dr. Otazo speaks from having *seen* what works—and what doesn't—across thousands of her client managers. This is a very readable, practical manual, chock full of savvy insights and advice."
—*Brad Smart, Author of* **Topgrading,** *www.topgrading.com*

"Dr. Otazo has allowed the 'Divine' to enrich, bless, and empower us with detailed insights that make a difference. Simple tenets for complex times. Elegant prose, proficient wit, sweet charm, and tried and tested expertise is what the global business community needs...now. Like an ancient sage of old, her still gentle prophetic voice crying loud from the wilderness of information clutter and foolishness will guide us. Leaders will sing a 'new song' in a strange land."
—*Dr. Alvin Augustus Jones, CEO, Be*

THE TRUTH
ABOUT BEING A
LEADER

FINANCIAL TIMES

In an increasingly competitive world, it is quality
of thinking that gives an edge—an idea that opens new
doors, a technique that solves a problem, or an insight
that simply helps make sense of it all.

We work with leading authors in the various arenas
of business and finance to bring cutting-edge thinking
and best-learning practices to a global market.

It is our goal to create world-class print publications
and electronic products that give readers
knowledge and understanding that can then be
applied, whether studying or at work.

To find out more about our business
products, you can visit us at www.ftpress.com.

THE TRUTH ABOUT BEING A LEADER ...AND NOTHING BUT THE TRUTH

Dr. Karen Otazo

An Imprint of Pearson Education

London • New York • San Francisco • Toronto • Sydney
Tokyo • Singapore • Hong Kong • Cape Town • Madrid
Paris • Milan • Munich • Amsterdam

Vice President and Editor-in-Chief: Tim Moore
Acquisitions Editor: Paula Sinnott
Editorial Assistant: Susie Abraham
Development Editor: Russ Hall
Associate Editor-in-Chief and Director of Marketing: Amy Neidlinger
Cover Designer: Sandra Schroeder
Managing Editor: Gina Kanouse
Senior Project Editor: Lori Lyons
Copy Editor: Gayle Johnson
Senior Compositor: Gloria Schurick
Proofreader: Debbie Williams
Manufacturing Buyer: Dan Uhrig

© 2007 by Pearson Education, Inc.
Publishing as FT Press
Upper Saddle River, New Jersey 07458

FT Press offers excellent discounts on this book when ordered in quantity for bulk
purchases or special sales. For more information, please contact U.S. Corporate
and Government Sales, 1-800-382-3419, corpsales@pearsontechgroup.com.
For sales outside the U.S., please contact International Sales at
international@pearsontechgroup.com.

Printed in the United States of America

First Printing November 2006

ISBN 0-13-187338-5

Pearson Education LTD.
Pearson Education Australia PTY, Limited.
Pearson Education Singapore, Pte. Ltd.
Pearson Education North Asia, Ltd.
Pearson Education Canada, Ltd.
Pearson Educatión de Mexico, S.A. de C.V.
Pearson Education—Japan
Pearson Education Malaysia, Pte. Ltd.

Library of Congress Cataloging-in-Publication Data
Otazo, Karen L.
   The truth about being a leader : and nothing but the truth / Karen Otazo.
       p. cm.
   Includes bibliographical references and index.
   ISBN 0-13-187338-5 (hardback : alk. paper) 1. Leadership. I. Title.
   HD57.7.O83 2006
   658.4'092—dc22

2005037737

CONTENTS

Contents

Contents

FOREWORD

As an executive coach, author, and keynote speaker, I am constantly on the lookout for books I can recommend to clients and readers that will help them to understand the most fundamental principles of leadership. Each year I read hundreds of books and articles on the topic with the hope that they will provide an honest and practical approach to a challenge many people accept with little or no training, guidance, or support. *The Truth About Being a Leader* is the book I often search for and rarely find.

That's one reason why I was delighted to write a preface for this book. Another reason is because I am intimately familiar with Dr. Karen Otazo's knowledge and approach to leadership development. Karen coached, mentored, and supported me when I was just starting my consulting practice two decades ago. Always on the cutting edge of professional development, she introduced me to the world of business coaching at a time when most people had never even heard of it. She allowed me to cofacilitate leadership workshops with her, where I learned about concepts and theories I myself had never thought of. And when I balked at conducting a training program in which I had no previous experience, she gave me an outline and insisted I could do it and do it well. In short, she was the ideal coach for a neophyte consultant and now, in this book, she uses her wisdom and insights to coach *you* on how to be a leader in *real time*.

I use the term *real time* because so many authors of leadership books are long on theory and short on practical, immediately useful advice. Among the many lessons I learned from Karen was the importance of providing people with coaching suggestions they can actually see in their mind's eye. She taught me to pretend I had a video camera trained on the person I was coaching. If the camera couldn't see it or hear it, then the person was less likely to be able to implement the advice. *The Truth About Being a Leader* does just that. Karen's words are so clear and concise that you can actually see or hear yourself engaging in the behavior she suggests. You, the reader, are the beneficiary of her lifetime of experiences as an organizational development executive and global coach.

There's one more thing I learned from Karen that this book underscores: that's the importance of having the courage to speak the unspoken. In this book she shares with you the true secrets of leadership success that are frequently overlooked in favor of the theory du jour written by the latest leadership guru. As hard as it may be to hear, she's right when she suggests "when you reach the top, you cannot afford to be too open with anyone inside or close to your organization." It may not be politically correct to assert "There are times in life, and the workplace, when a little bit of bullshit, or BS, is a good thing," but Karen's right about that, too. In fact, every one of her 52 short, pointed chapters speak the truth. She may not tell you what you *want* to hear—but it is surely what you *need* to hear.

Just as there is no one right diet to help all people lose weight, one right way to raise children, or one right method for preparing your Thanksgiving turkey, there is no one right way to lead. You should be very suspect of anyone who tells you they have the answers to all of your leadership challenges. In true Karen Otazo fashion, she doesn't pretend to have the magic formula for leadership success. Instead, as she did with me, she gives you lots of things to think about, on-target tips for how to be better tomorrow than you are today, and the confidence that you *can* be a great leader. Regardless of where you are on your leadership journey, you will find, as I did, that this book an invaluable addition to your leadership library.

Lois P. Frankel, Ph.D.

ACKNOWLEDGMENTS

I would like to thank the following people for their support and contributions to this book. Pearson Prentice Hall: Tim Moore, Paula Sinnott, Russ Hall, Lori Lyons, Lisa Berkowitz, Stephen Crane, and the editors and staff. Colleagues and friends: Lois Frankel, Colleen O'Brien, Michael Neill, Nicole Isaac, Lonnie Pacelli, Fran Mainella, Tom and Kellie Bartlett, and to the many global leaders who have shown me the way. Special thanks to my thinking partner, Daisy Froud.

ABOUT THE AUTHOR

Dr. **Karen Otazo** is a global executive coach and thinking partner for executives in multinational organizations as well as a leader of seminars for groups interested in maximizing their potential at work. More than 25 years of working in the U.S., China, India, Indonesia, Hong Kong, the UK, the Netherlands, France, Belgium, and Singapore, have given her a broad perspective on the challenges facing executives in companies of all sizes from boutique consulting firms or start-up non-profits to global corporations, joint ventures, and strategic alliances.

Her results-oriented approach has enabled her to build a blue chip client list that includes Ahold, AlliedSignal, American National Can, Amgen, ARCO, Avery Dennison, BankBoston, Booz Allen Hamilton, Central London Partnership, Chase Bank, Colgate-Palmolive, Colliers, CSFB, Digital, The Economist Group, FMC, Skanska Gammon Construction, General Electric, GlobalOne, Global Marine, Goldman Sachs, Hongkong Land, IBM, Ikea, Jardine Matheson, Lehman Brothers, Marks & Spencer, Motorola, Pixelpark (Bertelsmann), Readers Digest, Schindler, Sprint International, Syngenta, Time/Fortune International, and Vodafone. Many assignments have drawn on her experience with trans-national subsidiaries, joint ventures, and alliances.

In 2006, Pearson Prentice Hall published *The Truth about Managing Your Career... and Nothing But the Truth*. Future writing includes the power of intention, attention, and focus at work worldwide.

INTRODUCTION

Leadership isn't just another step in your career; it's a leap across the great divide. Everything changes, even if you stay in the same place. The familiar halls of your organization become a foreign landscape as you navigate new power structures, new demands, and new expectations. Suddenly, you have become a new person: a leader. Your mission? To motivate, align, inform, guide, and support your organization, through good times and bad.

It's easy to think that great leadership is some kind of innate ability or gift, to think that either you have it or you don't. That's not the case. Leadership gurus agree that great leaders are formed through their experiences, not born that way. Nevertheless, leadership is a tough act to jump into without some guidelines. This book gives you the necessary guidance to get you through the hard work, but also a few conjuring tricks or sleights of hand to help you in sticky situations. The good news is that a little effort goes a long way.

Think of the 52 short, to-the-point chapters in this book as a deck of cards. You can read and use them in any order. Riffle through the deck and draw what you need to build a strong hand. Use them to stay on your toes, playing one when you need to freshen your thinking. Whether you're a new graduate or an established leader, the truths in this book will help you consider where you are in your career and what else you want to accomplish.

For more than two decades, I have worked with hundreds of leaders worldwide, and I've learned that all leadership situations have truths in common. This book points out the pitfalls and shows you how to avoid them. It levels with you about the challenges of leadership, even those that people are reluctant to discuss. It will be your guide through one of the most challenging and rewarding transitions you'll ever make. You'll learn from the real-life challenges and successes of those who have made the leap.

You are a great doer, or you wouldn't have made it this far. To be a great leader, you need to learn a new game. *The Truth About Being a Leader* will help you master that game and play it so well that it will look like magic.

PART I

THE TRUTH ABOUT ASSUMING A LEADERSHIP POSITION

TRUTH 1

MORE-RESPONSIBLE ROLES REQUIRE MORE MENTAL "BANDWIDTH"

Leadership is a complex mix of responsibilities and account-abilities. To lead effectively, you need to be able to process large amounts of information quickly and handle multiple tasks at once. In computer terms, you need a lot of "bandwidth."

As you move up in leadership, you may start to feel that your processing speed is slowing down. The greater demands of a new position can expose areas in which your skills are not fully developed. This is not a cause for alarm, but a positive leadership challenge. The trick is to address those areas immediately, before they steal too much mental bandwidth from other vital parts of your job.

The following seven areas require your constant attention:

1. **Your personal work habits,** including keeping track of requests and commitments at meetings, your schedule, and follow-up with your team and others.

2. **Your personal mood and stress management**. Your moods affect many other people once you are in a senior position. As a leader, you need to do whatever it takes to respond with objectivity to the many demands on your

time and judgment so that your stress doesn't spread across the organization.

3. **Your leadership infrastructure and systems,** which include how you deal with your budget(s); your support staff; your organization's support functions, such as finance, human resources, and IT; and your organization's operations functions, such as sales, marketing, and manufacturing.

4. **Your vision and strategy.** These need to be developed over time so that they have the clarity and richness that stimulate others to move in the right direction. Whereas management is about avoiding the problems you encounter en route, leadership requires you to chart a string path forward for others.

> *As a leader, you need to do whatever it takes to respond with objectivity to the many demands on your time and judgment.*

5. **Your relationships with your leadership team members.** Good working relationships are the most effective way for you to implement your leadership agenda.

6. **Your relationships with peers and colleagues.** These impact upon the goodwill and trust that are vital for effective working. Cross the white space on your organization chart by connecting with others and keeping them informed.

7. **Your relationship with your boss,** whether a board, a matrix of bosses, or just one, is crucial to your success. (But no more so than any of the other areas, so beware of the temptation to attend to your boss(es) before all else!)

Inability to focus at meetings, getting easily frustrated, not attending to important follow-up, and ignoring key players are all signs that you're overwhelmed by your job, and that your bandwidth needs attention.

The easiest way to broaden your bandwidth is to strengthen your support systems. Can you designate someone as your second-in-command? Having such a person, known colloquially as your "2IC," is not only important for you but also a great learning opportunity for a direct report.

But don't make the same mistake as the leader who selected a business manager several rungs below him. The manager wound up filling in for his boss in situations that were way over his head, with negative consequences. It's vital for your own credibility that the people you use are right for their positions.

Remember that all areas of your leadership role need your attention. Neglected areas will inevitably trip you up when the demands of your new role put your bandwidth to the test.

TRUTH 2

INHERITING AN ASSISTANT REQUIRES REEDUCATION

If you inherit an assistant from your predecessor, you have to tread carefully in establishing this important relationship.

It is a mistake to underestimate your assistant or secretary's loyalty to the previous incumbent in your job—and to what he or she believes the company is or should be—as compared to his or her initial loyalty to you. You might think you "butter your assistant's bread," but you are the newcomer. In a sense, you are part of a "hostile takeover," since your assistant probably did not have a say in your taking over the role. If you don't concentrate on the relationship early on, you will be in trouble.

But if you get your assistant on your side, he or she will be your biggest support in a crunch. Your assistant can run interference for you and be in the "end zone" when needed. So, deal with your assistant first and in a different way from how you deal with the rest of your team.

How you deal with your assistant will vary depending on your style, his or her style, and which scenario you're faced with when starting the job. Here are three scenarios that the new relationship may present to you:

1. **When you come into the job, your assistant is already on your side and supports you completely, since "the boss is the boss."** Convincing is not the problem; rewarding is the way you need to think. If you don't notice and thank your assistant, he or she may not stay on your side for long. If you don't offer rewards like a bonus, flowers, lunch, working to get rid of jobs the person doesn't want, the relationship is one-sided and thus unstable.

2. **Your assistant is suspicious of you and waits to see who you are and how you treat people.** You're being tested. You'll recognize this situation when your assistant's behavior seems inconsistent. Sometimes you'll think your assistant is on your side, and other times you'll wonder why you were left out to dry instead of being given a heads-up on something. You need to reward your assistant when he or she is there for you and especially for giving you warnings and guidance. When your assistant fails to meet your expectations, express your disappoint-ment and ask for a different set of behaviors in the future. The key is that once you have asked for the new behavior, you need to move on and not dwell on it so that you re-educate rather than reject as you keep the air clear.

> *It is a mistake to underestimate your assistant's or secretary's loyalty to the previous incumbent in your job.*

3. **You find yourself with someone who has a limited view of the job, its relationship to you, the role that he or she has in giving you fair warnings, and the loyalty required in the way you are talked about**. In this case, you need to take more serious action. If you have repeatedly asked your assistant to leave 20 minutes between appointments so that you can regroup and prepare, but he or she consistently does not do so, several things may be happening. It might be better if he receives your instructions in writing. She may be pressured from the outside to schedule your time to meet other people's needs. He may only do things the way he's always done them and can only stay in a groove. She may be undermining you. For the last two, you have to deal with facts, not feelings. How frequently and to what degree does your assistant not follow directions? In an objective and unemotional way, you need to lay out the facts as you see them, along with your expectations and requirements. And you need to do this as a time-out rather than in ongoing coaching.

It's vital that you understand what your assistant is doing. Don't just get angry because he or she is not doing things the way you want. The key is to be objective, since most people fluctuate in their skills and commitment. If you find yourself with someone who believes there are areas that are "not my job," you need hard facts about what happened to ensure your objectivity.

The relationship with your assistant is important. Paying attention to that relationship early on increases the effectiveness and efficiency of your working together. If you find that it's not working because you have someone stuck in a groove who can't adjust, you should think about getting someone in the job who can work with you.

TRUTH 3

STAFFING YOUR LEADERSHIP OFFICE: YOUR ASSISTANT PLAYS A VITAL ROLE

Many of the people you'll deal with as a leader start forming their opinions of you long before you meet them—when they first call or visit your office and encounter your assistant. This person serves as an advertisement for who you are in your organization. If he or she is kind and gracious yet sets good boundaries, others will see professionalism.

Therefore, hiring the right assistant should be a top priority as you enter your leadership role, and the process needs your personal attention. It's a big mistake to leave the selection of such a key person to your office manager or someone in human resources. Others can help screen and process candidates, but it's your job to get your requirements straight and to conduct the final interviews.

Why is it worth taking the time to do this? Aren't all good assistants the same? No! Different people need different assistants!

Think about what you'd like—and we're not talking looks, age, or other vital statistics. Brainstorm a list of requirements, and put them in writing. Include the few characteristics that are required, the many that you would like to have, and the ones that you know will not work. Do you want someone who instantly responds to any request from senior executives, or do you need someone who talks with you each day and thinks through your requirements so that a senior executive request may get a bit of postponement? These are both valid approaches, yet are different ways of working.

Some common requirements may include hiring someone who

- Knows when to contact you when you are on the road.
- Screens your calls.
- Knows how to take into account your work pace and preferences when scheduling your diary.
- Shows loyalty by speaking well of you and keeping a professional distance with other colleagues and staff members.
- Thinks ahead to anticipate what you need.
- Checks for unforeseen problems that can result from everyday decisions.
- Is well connected in the company or can make connections quickly.

Once you've established your requirements, send your wish list to the HR team. Then choose the most qualified of the candidates they choose for interviews. And don't forget internal candidates so that you are fair and can compare.

Aren't all good assistants the same? No! Different people need different assistants!

Now think through your interview approach. How will you confirm candidates' abilities and make sure that their mind-sets match what you require for the job? The interview process may be dictated by the norms in your company, but it's your responsibility to get what you think you need.

The following techniques are all proven ways of drawing out a candidate's abilities. Use them individually, or combine them for really incisive interviews.

1. Ask candidates to **talk about what they did in every job they have had since school or at least in the last two to four positions. What did they enjoy most,** and which areas were not so enjoyable? What were they good at?

   What they enjoyed is a key to where their strengths lie. This helps you determine whether they have had experiences that will be useful in working with you.

2. As candidates talk about the positions they've held, ask **what they thought of previous bosses' strengths and weaknesses** (one or two of each will do). You're not asking them to be disloyal but to look at each boss objectively, since everyone has strengths and weaknesses. You're looking for what may apply to you. If you want someone who can think for himself, it should sound alarm bells if he says his former boss's strength was that she told him exactly what to do. If someone tells you that her boss gave her a lot of praise, do you want to do that consistently?

3. **Ask about hypothetical situations** based on your wish-list requirements. Is there something special about the job

you need done regularly? If so, compose a test situation. If you want to find out if someone can handle ambiguous scheduling requirements, pose a hypothetical situation: "What would you do if I were out of town and someone insisted on making an appointment for when I got back?"

4. **Acknowledging expectations.** Tell the candidates your expectations, and ask them to give you theirs. These expectations are good clues as to what they want in a job and whether they match your requirements.

Getting the right person to represent you to the world and to be a partner in your day-to-day work life can make or break your success in your leadership role. Taking the time to identify, check out, and hire that person is worth every hour and day you devote to the task. You will reap the benefits.

TRUTH 4

THE GAPS IN YOUR WORK HABITS SHOW UP WHEN YOU MOVE UP

Moving into leadership is like moving up in school. No matter how smart and motivated you are, if you don't know how to organize yourself, the complexity of your new environment will overwhelm you.

You probably advanced because you were the best at what you did. But what got you to where you are may not work anymore. In the past, you may have been able to "wing it" by relying on your wits, but the higher you go on the organizational chart, the more complicated things get.

George unexpectedly moved up from managing 12 salesmen to leading all his company's sales and marketing employees. A smart and enthusiastic leader, he found that he could no longer do what he used to do, which was drift around his department as he cajoled, praised, and pumped up his 12 people. Now he had 29 direct reports and a total of 400 people reporting to him. The little things he used to do, like going out with some of his team members for happy hour, didn't go down well with his new team.

Your new leadership position will require you to hone your **personal work habits:**

■ **Keep up with scheduling.** Ensure that you or someone who works for you puts every appointment and meeting on your calendar and that you show up on time.

■ **Delegate using quality standards and due dates.** Give your staff enough guidance and time to get their work done, and then hold them to their deadlines.

■ **Follow up on delegation and commitments.** Have your assistant keep a follow-up file so that you are on top of all delegated assignments.

■ **Make decision-making clear.** Let others know if your decisions include them and whether they have input into your decisions. Also let them know when a decision is theirs to make.

■ **Follow the money.** Have someone keep track of budget figures and expenditures on a monthly basis and balance the inflow and outflow.

You advanced because you were the best at what you did. But what got you to where you are may not work anymore.

■ **Ensure fairness in all you say and do.** Use checklists to keep track of which staff members you compliment or coach so that you don't inadvertently ignore some of them.

■ **Let go of being one of the guys.** Find leader-like and appropriate ways to interact in your new role. Spend time with your team and colleagues at meetings and meals. You need to forge a new way of working with others that is based on your leadership status, and sometimes that means maintaining some distance from your group.

Unless you invest enough time and thought into setting up effective working systems and relationships early on, you will get into bad habits and will never be able to advance very far. You'll get overwhelmed, like George, by the complexity, the meetings, and your inability to control the details you used to attend to. And the better you were at doing your job before, the more frustrated you will be about not being able to do what you used to do. Moving up as a leader involves a lot of letting go while still guiding others with interest and support. The sooner you stop doing parts of your old job and embrace the complexity of your new job, the more effective you will become.

TRUTH 5

A RESOURCE-BASED VIEW OF YOUR ORGANIZATION GOES BEYOND THE NUMBERS

Keeping an eye on resources is essential to managing any organization, even a household. Yet some people are still surprised to suddenly find that their cupboards are bare or their bank accounts have no money because they haven't been watching the inflow and outflow of their resources.

When you move into a new leadership position, you naturally think to check on your organization's tangible resources: financials like revenues and costs, factories, buildings, equipment, systems, inventory, patents, and land. But it is also vital to realize that less-obvious resources like customers, learning, staff, innovation, capacity, inventory control, and morale can make or break your organization's success.

Think of each resource as a bathtub with two valves—one bringing in the elements of that resource, and one draining them. If the resource is staff, the in-valve is regular hiring, and the out-valve is staff leaving. If you don't pay attention to hiring and focused career development, you may find yourself with a depleted resource of good staff.

If you're developing more business, or new kinds of business, looking at the bathtub called staff forces you to consider how much inflow you need to be ready to staff new areas as they come up. Even if times are tough, it's best to make sure your important resources don't drain away to a critical level. It is a common mistake not to hire new people when you have a bad year or are short of funds. In cyclical industries like the oil business that have boom and bust cycles, when a downturn is over it becomes almost impossible to find people to staff the emerging boom.

Thinking of your resources as bathtubs helps you see that resources move in and out all the time. So you need to keep an eye on the level in every one of your tubs and ensure that you're putting enough into each of them.

How do you identify all your bathtubs (resources)? You can get your team together, perhaps with some outside players like customers, consultants, and your board, to determine what makes your organization special. Open your thinking to the less-tangible resources as well as the obvious ones. For instance, you might not think of morale as a resource. Or brand. You might need to have a brainstorming exercise to determine what all your tubs are—all the things that make your organization what it is. These might include the people, the location, the value proposition of the product or

> *Thinking of your resources as bathtubs helps you see that resources move in and out all the time.*

service offered, and the advertising. Then determine what causes inflow and outflow for each resource.

For the resources of customers and learning, the tubs might look like this:

Customers Inflow	Outflow
Potential customers	Dissatisfied customers
Rivals' customers	Customers attracted to another organization
Newly attracted customers	Attracted customers who don't then use products or services

Learning Inflow	Outflow
Training and development	Haphazard learning
Knowledge management	Lack of knowledge management
Hiring experienced personnel	Loss of key personnel

One important bathtub is reputation. Reputations can't be measured in numbers, but you certainly know if you have a good or bad one. When you realize that your reputation has drained below the "good" line, you can work on it. But first you have to realize this!

In gauging the levels of each of your tubs, you need to do fact-finding. Otherwise, you're using the intuition and feelings of just a few people. For instance, you can check on morale by doing a climate survey or check on customer attitudes with focus groups. Getting solid information from surveys and staff readiness reports from your leaders gives you a foundation for your decisions about where to support designated resources.

Taking a real resource-based view, rather than just getting a few facts and figures, is important. It's also tricky, because a lot of these things can't be measured in a bean-counting way. But, as with a bath, you don't have to count the gallons of water. What's important is whether your tub is comfortably full or worryingly empty.

PART II

THE TRUTH ABOUT EFFECTIVE LEADERSHIP STYLES

TRUTH 6

SOFT-SPOKEN LEADERSHIP REQUIRES STAMINA

When we think about great leaders, we tend to think of the extroverts—those who speak engagingly and freely about their visions. Perhaps you compare yourself unfavorably to these exemplars. For example, perhaps you responded to an important question from a staff member only after a long, uncomfortable silence. Or maybe you felt uncomfortable or at a loss for words in front of a large audience. You may have worried that you weren't up to the job. Well, don't jump to conclusions!

Although extrovert leaders get publicity and are celebrated by popular leadership books, research has shown that a less conspicuous, more measured style of leadership can work equally well. Professor Jim Collins, in his 2001 book *Good to Great*, found that some of the most effective leaders don't have a high media profile. They show their strengths in other ways: by just getting things done, cleanly and firmly.

Successful quiet leadership means taking Teddy Roosevelt's advice to speak softly and carry a big stick. Your "big stick" is a combination of stamina and determination. You know where you're going, and you've thought carefully about what you need to do to get there; you just don't make a song and dance about it. This low profile can be far more valuable to an organization than lots of noise and enthusiasm. But you need to work extra hard to get your leadership message out there.

Collins found that even Abraham Lincoln was initially misunderstood because his peaceful demeanor hid his resolve to preserve the Union. Quiet leaders like Colman M. Mockler, CEO of Gillette, transformed their companies in the face of opposition, keeping their eyes on future greatness as opposed to present acclaim. Mockler lead Gillette from 1975 to 1991. He doggedly moved his company forward to dominate the markets until he died. His vision has lived on.

As a soft-spoken leader, what key moves help you play to your strengths?

1. **Keep it personal.** You are likely to work a lot better one-on-one or in small groups of people you know. This allows you to focus your energy on one person at a time. If you have to meet with a larger group, set aside time to connect with individual participants in advance. Use those conversations to lobby people and get buy-in for your ideas, rather than running a meeting "as it comes." Follow up on any decisions with people individually afterward.

2. **Take your time before acting.** Before launching a new initiative, successful leaders tend to carefully consider the resources needed to deliver it. They also think carefully about what challenges they might encounter on the way. Such preparation is not glamorous, but it is highly effective. It's particularly important for those of a quieter

temperament, because it allows you to build a solid case for action that will stand up to the questions of more vociferous colleagues. Taking time to have internal dialogues may initially confuse or frustrate others, but they'll appreciate the results and will come to trust your approach.

3. **Prepare well before speaking.** When it comes to key meetings and

Taking time to have internal dialogues may initially confuse or frustrate others, but they'll appreciate the results and will come to trust your approach.

presentations, spontaneous speaking probably is not your strong suit. Again, you'll do best when you give yourself plenty of time to plan. Choose presentation formats that suit your preferences by opting for meetings with many small groups rather than a few large ones whenever possible. It's also helpful to write out your presentation in detail so that if you get stage fright you can glance at your notes to get things back on track.

With preparation, quiet leaders are steady and reliable contributors who make an impact. If you have "quiet" people working for you, don't underestimate them. And if you are a quiet leader, don't underestimate yourself!

TRUTH 7

BULLSHIT MAKES GOOD FERTILIZER—
JUST WATCH YOUR STEP

In his recent best seller *On Bullshit*, Harry G. Frankfurt writes: "One of the most salient features of our culture is that there is so much bullshit." You may feel that this is all too true. From media, to politicians, to colleagues at work, at times it can seem that everyone around you has developed an unhealthy disregard for the value of honesty. But hold your horses! (Or should that be your bulls?) There are times in life, and in the workplace, when a little bit of bullshit, or BS, is a good thing.

BS in the negative sense is something suspiciously smelly. Deceitful or boastful language is certainly not something to be encouraged in the workplace. However, there is a place for BS when you're conjecturing about the future or developing ideas. It makes good fertilizer, helping ideas grow by bringing out the best in them. But it's important to know what that place is and to keep the BS confined to it. A little bit of BS does you and the organization good. Too much can confuse people, make them distrust you, or unduly raise their expectations about what is possible. So make sure you give others clear signals when your words aren't meant to be taken literally.

Here are the principal circumstances where BS works:

1. **Brainstorming.** If your team isn't worried about backing up every idea with solid plans, they may be able to think more creatively and approach problems in novel ways. So, when imagining ideal or possible outcomes, or laying the groundwork for a new initiative, such as an advertising campaign, make sure everyone knows that the sky's the limit. Before starting a brainstorming session, let everyone know that nothing is set in stone or has to be acted on. Any numbers mentioned aren't real until approved. This is key for the logical and financially minded. They don't like to see faked numbers, even when the numbers are designed to jog your thinking.

2. **Selling an idea.** When you want to sell something or bring people on board, mild exaggeration is allowed. You need to present your work in the best possible light. Good

> *A little bit of BS does you and the organization good.*

marketers create the most amazing promotional material. If you know the facts, you may read this material thinking, "That can't be true." But when you analyze it, you see it's just polished to look bigger and better than reality. If you were teasing the marketer, you might accuse him of bullshitting, but he is just doing a very good job! Even endorsements on the backs of books have a bit of BS in them. When they don't, these blurbs may fall flat.

3. **Relaxing others.** A little hot air can also ease stress in social situations you encounter at work. Wisecracks, tall stories, and jocular empty talk can help create a fun and informal atmosphere, letting others know that it's time to relax and transition from work to play. It's essential, though, to carefully tailor your BS to the audience to ensure that you do not cause offense or get misinterpreted.

4. **Scenario planning.** This is the science of imagining the future. Participants, often working with a consultant, set up and play out possible future scenarios, bringing in possible and improbable events to plan for how an organization will react to them and manage them. An example is exploring the consequences for your company's substantial business in China if that country were to go to war with India. The more creative a story you can tell, the better, in this kind of organizational exercise.

Whether you call it BS, blarney, or poetic license, there are times when a little exaggeration can play a positive role in organizational life. It can give you and others freedom to play around with ideas and to ease the strictures of corporate culture. And that's no bullshit!

TRUTH 8

PLAYER/COACH IS A TRICKY ROLE, SO MAKE SURE THAT YOU DO BOTH WELL

Some of the most admired actors, like Clint Eastwood and Robert Redford, moved from acting to directing their own movies. They learned to juggle the duties of lead actors while being responsible for the entire production. The same thing happens in sports when the best players serve as coaches for their teams while playing in games.

Player/coach is a common term for a similar role in organizations. The player/coach is in charge of what his or her team does but also regularly has to perform the same work as the team. Producer/manager positions are common, for example, in the fields of sales and training. Often the leader "plays" as well, either because there aren't enough other players or because the business at stake is so important that the best player's skills are needed. These blurred boundaries create a challenge. The leader is put into a position where he or she must play both roles. Where do you put your energy and focus to optimize the results for your team? When should you focus on being a player, and when on being a manager?

It's probably true that you attained your leadership position because you were the best at what you did. It can therefore be hard to let go when you know that you'll make better decisions, get things done faster, and score better than your team members. However, on a day-to-day basis, you should work to keep the emphasis on your coaching role, stepping in to play only when it is essential.

When you do step in, it is important to resist the temptation to be the star player, outshining your colleagues and putting their achievements in the shade, even if this leads to victory in the short term. Such behavior disempowers your team members by possibly making them feel inadequate and by setting a precedent where they look to you for success rather than creating their own. It also means that you are likely to miss out on others' thinking and creativity. If the post-success glory is focused on you, team members may additionally feel resentment at your star role.

What about times when you are required to play? A good player/coach heeds the following advice, making sure that your skills and talents are used to best effect and to the benefit of both team and organization:

- **Share your thinking.** When you are in player mode, make sure that you include fellow players in the decisions you make, showing them how to construct and deliver an effective strategy, and discussing the options with them when possible. By explaining your thinking, you successfully coach at the same time, modeling the way for the team with guideposts. You'll find that the more you share with your team, the more they will learn how to think for themselves.

■ **Weigh the needs of each situation.** Some circumstances demand your participation more than others. These include the following occasions:

The more you share with your team, the more they will learn how to think for themselves.

Your boss expects you to make the score on your own. Sometimes a boss may want to know that you made it happen through your knowledge and skills or your relationship with top leaders. That's part of his or her coaching you, so go with it.

A special relationship is at stake. Business with key clients or partners may benefit from your intervention. Be careful, though, not to prevent your team members from developing such relationships with important clients.

A unique ability will give your team the advantage. If you have a particular skill or specialty that will help clinch a deal, it's worth bringing it into play. This might be the ability to close a sale or gain the approval of a key political support.

■ **Think ahead.** When you weigh whether to play or lead, think through the implications of your actions. When you have the option of playing or coaching, the long-term payoff is often greater in the coach role.

You're already a great player. As a player/coach, you now have the opportunity to be a great leader—at least some of the time!

TRUTH 9

CARING LEADERS TREAT THEIR TEAMS LIKE FAMILY

Ever gone to a family dinner where the kids had their own table? They may have the same tableware and food, but they feel left out of the action. The same thing can happen with your leadership family: they each want a seat at the table.

Your leadership family consists of all the leaders and managers who report to you. Not only do these people see themselves as your key players, but they want to be recognized as such. They also want you to support them and back them up—to be treated like family. You miss out on a great deal of potential if you fail to respect them in that way. Making people feel included and cared for encourages good communication and collective working—key ingredients of an integrated team. That's not to say that from time to time there won't be rivalries and conflicts, but on the whole a sense of family generates a climate in which coworkers support and cover for each other.

Mike, president of a medium-sized company, had six direct reports running the major business areas. Mike had great relationships with these folks. He spoke with them every day, sharing much of his strategizing. These leaders had 17 direct reports between them. Mike's relationship was very different with this second tier of managers.

When talking one day about a new initiative with a member of this second tier, Mike was surprised to find out that she didn't have a clue what he was talking about. Probing deeper, he realized that many of his managers didn't know important elements of his strategy. They had also started to feel as though they didn't matter, excluded from the information loop. When Mike raised this with his immediate team, they protested that they didn't have time to communicate all his messages.

So Mike took action. He introduced a quarterly group update with all 23 managers so that everyone could hear his leadership messages directly from him. They also could feed back their news, opinions, and accomplishments. Between gatherings, Mike met informally with team members to get their opinions on, and judge their reactions to, organizational strategy. He also met weekly with his immediate reports as a group and often one-on-one as well.

Making people feel included and cared for encourages good communication and collective working.

This new approach not only helped Mike convey his agenda, but it also helped him understand where each of the 23 leaders wanted to excel and could best contribute. The leaders themselves better understood what was happening in the company and the reasons why. Their energy and commitment increased. The immediate reports still felt privileged as the "older, more responsible" family members, not bypassed by the new system, since Mike made it clear that he was supporting their communication, not replacing it.

Mike ensured that his leadership family benefited from these key behaviors that are essential to a healthy leadership family:

1. **Ongoing, up-to-date communication** from the head of the family to family members about organizational news and strategy.

2. **Ongoing feedback** encouraged and facilitated between family members and the head of the family, ensuring that their opinions are taken into account.

Do you need to be the equivalent of a warm and caring parent all the time? Absolutely not! You are not in business to be loving or affectionate.

An organizational "sense of family" is about treating people as professionals, but also as individuals who are respected and cared for. Communication flow in both directions is well worth the investment. You'll soon see the increase in loyalty and commitment.

TRUTH 10

INNOVATION REQUIRES PREPARATION

A century ago, Thomas Edison thought deeply about what drives invention or, as we call it today, innovation. One of his famous sayings—"Genius is 1 percent inspiration and 99 percent perspiration"—stresses that innovation originates not in great ideas, but in the hard work of trial and error. Edison's inventions, like the light bulb and the phonograph, emerged through thousands of attempts, refining the process step by step.

Like Edison, you need to build innovation systematically into your leadership style to foster it in your organization. Like many apparently spontaneous workplace triumphs, good innovation is the result of well-planned project management or, more specifically, "process management." You often don't know precisely where you will end up, so you lead from behind, giving your team frequent feedback, encouraging them to stay positive and keep moving, testing, and refining their ideas as they gradually develop an outcome.

Nico, a leader in Indonesia and a natural innovator himself, found generating innovation in others more difficult. A forthright person, the more he demanded new ideas and products from his staff, the less they produced, and the less happy he was with their work. Nico gradually learned to spot when team members needed guidance and support, rather than just being left alone. Realizing that the creative freedom he delighted in was daunting, even paralyzing, to those who were less dynamic, he introduced a more structured approach to research and development. Before a new project, Nico would sit down with team members and think through the project's aims, as well as challenges or problems they might encounter along the way. He also helped his team stay on top of their game by setting up their work so that they could stay grounded and rested.

If it were simple and easy, it probably wouldn't be innovative.

The quality of leadership can make all the difference to innovation and creativity in organizations. To lead in the spirit of Edison, try the following process-oriented techniques to encourage innovative thinking:

- **Encourage your team to embrace mistakes.** Mistakes can actually aid the process of discovery and innovation if you accept them and learn from them. Mistakes provide the feedback for course corrections you need on your zigzag path to success. If it were simple and easy, it probably wouldn't be innovative.

- **Promote "messy thinking."** Allow your team to explore more than one path to solving problems. That freedom can open up productive lines of inquiry.

- **Invite contrary opinions.** If someone is critical of your approach, don't automatically defend it. Consider inviting that person into the process. Microsoft did just that when it invited its most virulent blogger to join the organization!

- **Consider using "skunkworks."** Sometimes a small group working outside the usual rules and management structure can get results quickly. The work might take place away from the office, or even in secret. Freeing your team from their normal constraints may help them move more confidently in a new direction.

- **Be a cheerleader as well as a coach.** Your staff members need support and enthusiasm as well as advice about how to deal with obstacles and challenging situations. Many times staff get discouraged when they hit what seem like dead ends. Keep them moving and positive.

Good innovation requires a focus on the process, not just specific outcomes or timelines. Keep the general needs of your consumers or beneficiaries in mind, but allow the process of exploration to lead to unexpected places. When you empower your employees to try new ideas and make mistakes along the way, you allow innovation to thrive in your organization.

PART III

THE TRUTH ABOUT WHAT YOU SAY AS A LEADER

TRUTH 11

MATCH YOUR LEADERSHIP MESSAGE TO YOUR AUDIENCE

W hen you're giving a presentation, do you ever wish you could look inside your audience's heads to see whether they're tuned in to what you're saying? In a way, scientists now can do that with magnetic resonance imaging (MRI). By looking at MRI brain scans, they have learned that different people's brains react differently to the same information, depending on the medium of the message.

Most people have a preferred way to take in information. Some prefer to hear it, some to see it, and some to touch or "get a feel" for it. By carefully observing someone, you can determine which approach works best for him or her. You can help that person focus more fully on your message by matching how you present information to the way he or she prefers to receive it.

Watch your audience members when you give a presentation to a small group. Eye movements can be a big clue. People who prefer to see information often stare off into space, visualizing your message. People who like to hear information frequently look to one side, with their heads tilted slightly. And people who need to get a feel for information often look down toward their dominant hand. They may doodle or make other movements like foot wiggling or might even get up to walk around when possible. Some psychobabble says people who wiggle their feet, don't make eye contact, or doodle while you talk are ignoring you. Nonsense. That's simply how their brains work.

If you need to communicate with a particular person, it's simple to tailor your information to his or her preferred type of message. For the visually oriented, bullet points, charts, and illustrations work well. For listeners, catchy language captures their attention. And for people who like to get a feel for things, try a model they can manipulate or a handout they can write on. Sometimes talking things over can also help people in this last group get a feel for your message.

Addressing a large group of people is trickier. As the saying goes, you can't please all of the people all of the time. However, by providing information in a variety of forms, you can give everyone something to focus on. A concise talk and accompanying slide show with moments for group discussion offer the necessary variety. Or, more strategically, you can target the medium used toward the preferred communication method of key audience members. It pays to ensure you don't turn them off.

> *By providing information in a variety of forms, you can give everyone something to focus on.*

When we receive information in our most preferred form, our brains enter "beta" mode—a highly focused state. This is what you want to induce in your audience. When we are less focused, our brains are more open to new ideas. This state, called "alpha," is a bit like daydreaming. When we are addressed via our least-preferred media input, our brains enter a meditative state called "theta." The openness of the alpha state and the calming theta mode are sometimes desirable when thoughtfully used. Aim to put yourself in beta mode when you need to concentrate, in alpha when you want to brainstorm and get creative, and in theta when you want to zone out and relax your brain. That's what a lot of people do when they go home and unwind. They are encouraging their brains to go into theta mode.

What goes for others goes for you too. It's worth working out your own preferences, perhaps by asking someone else to observe you. As a leader, don't forget to let other people know what works best for you. Then strive to pay attention!

TRUTH 12

IMPACTFUL LEADERS SPEAK SIMPLY

The most famous sound bite of Bill Clinton's first presidential campaign was "It's the economy, stupid." This was a variation on "KISS," a famous acronym for "Keep it simple, stupid." To lessen the insult factor, it's sometimes rendered as "Keep it simple and short" or "Keep it simple and straightforward."

Leaders who are experts in their fields are often tempted to fill their messages with more detail than necessary, resulting in a kind of intellectual "creep" that obscures what they're trying to say. Good software designers know that no matter how complex something is behind the scenes, the interface with the consumer must be simple. Your leadership speeches and talks are your consumer interface. The simpler and clearer you can make your message, the better it will be remembered.

It's the audience that matters, not the information! You may be accustomed to addressing other technical professionals like yourself, but when you move into leadership, your audience widens. Think through and practice what to say so that it comes across clearly to all your listeners. Whether you're making a presentation to a large group or giving instructions to one of your staff, a simple message is always the most understandable and memorable.

The irony of simplicity, though, is that it can take longer to be simple than to ramble and tell all you know. Take the time to focus, and **craft your message carefully:**

Good software designers know that no matter how complex something is behind the scenes, the interface with the consumer must be simple.

- ■ **Consider everyone's expectations.** What does your audience expect to learn from you? What key information do you need them to walk away with?

- ■ **Write out those expectations in headline form.** The audience's expectations are paramount, and yours are secondary.

- ■ Use the headlines to shape your message and **create your talking points.**

- ■ **Stick to the essentials.** Address the audience's expectations and cover your top ones, but not all of them. There is always more you could share, but adding lots of detail is the lazy way out.

- ■ **Offer your audience the chance to get more information,** either one-on-one or in writing, perhaps from a Web site or brochure.

The more often you prepare this way, the better you'll get at keeping it simple. But the only way to know for sure whether your message is getting across is to ask. Testing and trying out your material ahead of time ensures that you're ready. Feedback ensures that you'll do better next time.

Tone and volume are important too. Short sentences, punch and pause, and a low-pitched but clearly audible tone of voice that is easily heard make a powerful combination. Together they add up to the classic leader sound, known as "command tone." Generals, principals, teachers, and police all have it, and everyone knows that they are in charge.

Craft your sound bites well, and let them sizzle. As every restaurateur knows, people buy the sizzle, not the steak. They remember the excitement of the meal long after the taste is forgotten. Keep your sentences short, with lots of pause and punch. Whether they love you or hate you, they'll never forget what you said.

TRUTH 14

YOUR TONE OF VOICE SHOULD COMMAND ATTENTION

What do teachers, military officers, and other leaders have in common? They know how to use *command tone*. When they speak, others listen and want to follow them. Whether your audience is motivated or apathetic, a commanding tone lets you project your voice so that others hear you and respond.

Voice coaches help leaders create their own command tone to reinforce their leadership messages. Patsy Rodenburg, head of the voice department at London's Royal National Theatre, has coached many of the world's great actors, from Judi Dench to Olympia Dukakis, and politicians like Tony Blair. Her books and classes focus on how you can project yourself into your part with your voice. When an American came to Rodenburg for coaching on her leadership communication, she focused on two areas that would make an enormous difference for the executive: a commanding voice tone and crisp, clear enunciation.

■ **Command tone.** Think of your voice projecting to the other side of the room without a hint of shouting. Rodenburg maintains that a commanding voice happens when you breathe correctly from the abdomen. Barring an injury to the lower back, anyone can practice diaphragm breathing simply by letting the lower ribcage/stomach area expand with each breath. If you think of your voice as a sound projecting from inside your ribs, or abdomen area, rather than from your throat, your tone will be more commanding. It will also reach across the room without your shouting.

> *It's well nigh impossible to have crisp, clear pronunciation when you are rushed. Don't rush, no matter how little time you think you have.*

- **Crisp, clear enunciation.** You may feel silly at first, but exaggerating the clarity of how you say every word is a good way to prepare your communication. Rodenburg would have you practice carefully pronouncing each word of a famous poem so that the content ceases to matter and you can focus on the clarity of pronunciation. Justice Sandra Day O'Connor is said to have claimed that when she learned to enunciate clearly, she started to compete with men on an equal basis.

You'll find that it's well nigh impossible to have crisp, clear pronunciation when you are rushed. Don't rush, no matter how little time you think you have.

Command requires speaking with strength, energy, clarity, and crispness. Your leadership tone of voice has a huge impact on how others remember and respond to you. Practice your command tone and enunciation so that others will hear you and follow.

TRUTH 15

NAMES MATTER TO PEOPLE, SO GET THEM RIGHT

Sociologist Erving Goffman, who is famous for his work on impression management at work, wrote about life in U.S. mental institutions of the 1950s. He spoke of the institutional admission process as a dismantling of individuality. Inmates lost clothes, jewelry, and other personal possessions. However, the most significant loss was not physical. It was your name. Like other institutions, including prisons, what you most associate with—who you are—was taken away and replaced with a number.

Names matter. Your name is your identity. It's how others recognize you. It differentiates you from others and defines who you are. It follows that if you want to build strong and trusting working relationships, it pays to remember others' names and to spell and say them correctly. It's also important to pay attention to titles when applicable. In many parts of the world, you need to address people by their titles and last names as opposed to first names, until they suggest otherwise. In doing so, you set a good example for your followers.

Picture a gala dinner hosted by a top Fortune 500 company. The guest of honor, president of a South American country, is listening to the host company's president enthusiastically introduce him. Unfortunately, the host seems incapable of pronouncing his name. The guest winces every time his name is mispronounced. He then goes home early. The event, designed as a gracious gesture to honor the company and the president, winds up offending him instead. The outcome is that tens of thousands of dollars is wasted.

What could that top executive have done to avoid this situation, and what should you do if you don't want to fall into the same trap?

- **Do your research.** Get your staff to help find out how any unusual-looking name is pronounced. If the name originates in another country or culture, often someone in your organization will know how to say it. Alternatively, have someone call the person's office to find out how the name should be said.

- **Write down the name phonetically.** Even once you know a name, the pronunciation can be hard to remember. So write it down syllable by syllable in a way that makes sense to you and that allows you to pronounce it correctly. For instance, the name Otazo is pronounced *oh-tah-so* in Spanish.

- **Practice.** Work with someone who knows the name, saying it repeatedly, until the pronunciation comes naturally.

If you have trouble remembering names, try the following:

- **Ask people to repeat their names.** There's no shame in not remembering someone's name the first time you hear it, especially if it's unusual or if you are meeting lots of people. Simply ask someone, "What did you say your name was again?" or "Would you pronounce your name again for me?" Repetition helps names stick.

> *There's no shame in not remembering someone's name the first time you hear it, especially if it's unusual or if you are meeting lots of people.*

- **Ask a question about the name.** Rather than going on to another topic, build on your introduction to ask about the name's origins or spelling. Getting this context—the story around the name—helps fix it in your memory.

- **Use the name immediately.** As soon as you learn a name, look for opportunities to repeat it. Finish sentences with the name—"What do you think of the venue, Bob?"—and use it when you say goodbye.

■ **Write down the name.** If it's not an event where
you're swapping business cards, such as a gala dinner,
and you're meeting lots of people, have a staff member
write each name down as you learn it, along with some
distinguishing information. Immediately afterward, add
some notes about each person. Having a clear picture
of that person helps you remember who is who the
next time you meet.

In the words of Yahoo's Jerry Yang, "It helps a ton when
you learn people's names and don't butcher them when trying
to pronounce them." If you remember others' names, they feel
you care. Show them you do.

TRUTH 16

"COMING ATTRACTIONS" GET OTHERS TUNED IN TO YOUR MESSAGE

Hollywood studios know that they need to prepare their audiences by giving them a taste of the movie to come. They use advertising trailers to highlight the coming attractions. These mini-movies draw in an audience, making them eager to see more.

A similar approach is helpful when readying a work audience. A few carefully chosen extra words, before you launch into the thrust of your message, help engage your audience—whether that's one person or many—readying them for what you want them to remember, and giving their thinking a jump-start. I call this organizational version of coming attractions a "priming frame." It's a vital leadership technique. Offering some context to your message helps take your words beyond mere instructions. It helps others understand the what, why, and how of what they are about to do, empowering them to act swiftly and confidently.

The simplest priming frame is a set of verbal bullet points letting listeners know what topics you will cover: "Today we'll discuss a, b, c, d, and e. I'll spend about 3 to 5 minutes on each

Beginning with the purpose behind your request clearly sets the stage for your audience, emphasizing that the work they do for you is meaningful.

point." If you follow this with an explanation of why you are doing this—"This will allow us to systematize our project work over the next three months so that we'll all be on the same page as we move toward our overall goal"— your listeners will be absolutely clear about where you are going and how it relates to them, so they know to listen.

Here are the main messages that a priming frame should be used to convey:

1. The **agenda** of what you'll say
2. The **timing** of what you're telling or asking
3. The **purpose behind your request or comment**
4. The **vision or goals** that you've discussed before

The extended example just given efficiently achieves all four. Depending on your audience and your objectives, you should put more or less emphasis on one or the other at different times. **Agenda** and **timing** are straightforward to convey; you just give the facts. The other two benefit from a little more consideration.

Beginning with the **purpose behind your request** clearly sets the stage for your audience, emphasizing that the work they do for you is meaningful. The phrase "so that" is very useful here. It concisely indicates the overall rationale. "We're doing this so that we can make the deadline."

Referring to a previously discussed **vision or goals** is useful when asking something new or controversial. Your vision—a clear statement or set of principles shared by everyone—acts like a collective anchor to which you can then attach specific requests. Your "priming frame" should indicate how your new instructions are a way to further that vision.

For instance, suppose your organization has agreed that it needs to raise its profile through investing in corporate social responsibility initiatives, and an opportunity has arisen to prepare a bid to invest in a local public school mentoring scheme. The fact that you are asking the team to work overtime for the next week to pull together the bid makes sense. But you need to make that link explicit upfront, rather than just hoping that people will make the link for themselves: "A great opportunity has come up for us to make our corporate social responsibility target and really make a difference to the local community, but it will require some extra work from everyone." Asking people to work overtime on such short notice without tying it to a shared goal would just generate resentment.

"Priming frames" are a proven technique to help audiences tune in to your messages. Using them not just in person, but also in correspondence, helps ensure that you communicate successfully and avoid springing things on people. Your listeners will thank you and will be more likely to take action at your request.

PART IV

THE TRUTH ABOUT
LEADERSHIP VISION

TRUTH 17

WHAT'S THE BIG IDEA?
BRING YOUR GUIDING RULES INTO
EVERYDAY ORGANIZATIONAL LIFE

Our word *strategy* comes from the Greek *strategos*, meaning military general. This suggests that strategy is something that takes place at a high level. Although that may traditionally have been the case, in recent years the military, along with other organizations, has increasingly placed emphasis on empowering people at all levels. They take ownership of the organization's core values and strategy—its "big ideas"—and make decisions based on these daily.

If you want your staff to live by your organization's "big ideas," you must empower them to do so. You do this by communicating those ideas clearly. You also work out with them the practical ways in which they can live out those ideas every day so that they are fully part of your and their work. Don't just hand your employees a piece of paper to guide them; your core strategies need to be embedded within their consciousness.

It's one thing to have a sense yourself of where you want the organization to go; it's another to put those ideas into a form that others can share and identify with. You need to express two principles in clear, simple language that others can refer to in the course of their daily work. These are **how** you run this business—the guiding principles or rules of engagement that everyone needs to follow—and **where** you want the organization to go. For example, do you want your organization to have a higher profile in its market, to increase its customer base, or to increase profits by cutting expenses?

Don't just hand your employees a piece of paper to guide them; your core strategies need to be embedded within their consciousness.

What kind of day-to-day tactics can you use to accomplish these overall strategies? Let's look at an example of how the leader of one unusual organization—the Atlanta Braves—approached the challenge of being guided by its big ideas every day. The team's overall strategy is to develop and nurture a culture of winning. That's a bit like the goal of increasing shareholder value or making an organizational profitable. It's a wonderful end point to strive for.

The Braves' general manager established three big ideas to guide day-to-day decisions. Everything the team has done in 15 years of winning has been shaped by these ideas.

Big Idea 1: Everyone Needs to Be an "A" Player

Strategy: Move players in constantly and develop them; cull those who have lost the winning spark.

Everyday tactics:

1. Hire talent scouts to find the right players, construct and run player-development programs, and look at prospective players' abilities through tests and profiles.

2. Establish and hone athletic and mental skills needed, such as game toughness, confronting challenges, adaptability, and coachability.

Big Idea 2: Communicate with People About How They Are Doing

Strategy: Always show them respect, gratitude, and trust in their work.

Everyday tactics:

1. Communicate to the team that they are good and that they will produce.

2. Use your leadership confidence to bolster the team's confidence.

Big Idea 3: Use Real-World Evidence for Real-Time Feedback

Strategy: Use tangible, countable and visible evidence so that your players can clearly see what's happening.

Everyday tactic:

1. Use statistics to decide which players to bring in, to consistently adjust people's judgment and leverage their development, and to help everyone adapt to changes in their tactics in real time.

Work with your team to find the right big ideas for your organization by using the Atlanta Braves' work as a jumping-off point. Although they've never paid for a number-one draft choice, they consistently bring along their players through development and move out players who have peaked. Can you match that?

TRUTH 18

STORIES HELP MAKE CHANGE CLEAR

Once upon a time, there was a leadership tool. This tool was sharp and effective. It shaped followers' thinking, gave them insight into their organization's values and standards, and gave them a glimpse of the future. This tool was the story.

Stories, whether told at a child's bedside or in a boardroom, help listeners better understand life—as it is and as it might be. In the workplace, stories can help colleagues and staff understand the organization's norms, particularly when those are changing. People often find it hard to get their minds around new ideas and practices, especially when they threaten or disturb the status quo. Presenting change through the filter of a story can help you take people to an imaginative space outside daily life and allow them to consider the issues in a more objective way.

Think of stories as "scenarios." They depict the effects of possible events in personal and human terms. They put things in perspective in a way that people can relate to. If you feel awkward telling stories, it may help to picture the characters in your mind and make them real for yourself and hence for your audience. All kinds of stories can act as fables or parables to help others understand your ideas.

Here are some of the ways that stories can operate as a leadership tool:

- **Stories remove people from their everyday reality.** Like good movies and novels, stories are set in another world or context in which the challenges mirror those of real life. Listeners can absorb the core of your message without getting hung up on all the details that attend the literal situation. That can clear a path in their thoughts for change.

- **Stories are metaphors for what can happen in your organization.** A good story can prepare your followers to face a challenge. Like a Hollywood storyline, your story can evoke the excitement of overcoming an obstacle. Perhaps a story about the workers at Station X in World War II who broke the secret German code would illustrate your company's potential for phenomenal breakthroughs and your need for persistence. Or maybe a story from your organization's own past—of a moment when your predecessors decided to hunker down and turn things around—could connect your employees to the glory of that past. It could also show how each of them is a link in a chain that has endured many challenges and prospered.

- **Stories provide a clear hook that helps people see a vision or objective as real.** When you talk about major present or future challenges, or "burning platforms," you're talking about the need for change and about where your organization can go. Stories can help your listeners form a picture of where the change can lead them. The more you talk about clear and vivid imagined future situations, the more they are "remembered."

> *The more you talk about clear and vivid imagined future situations, the more they are "remembered."*

Whether stories are designed to explain a current economic situation or threats and opportunities in the future, telling stories can help your team deal with new realities by facing challenges in advance in their imaginations. When they have a chance to work out their thinking-through stories, they can better ready themselves for change.

TRUTH 19

PLAYING OUT THE TAPE HELPS OTHERS PREPARE FOR THE FUTURE

Since the advent of videotape and DVDs, we don't have to go to the movie theater or tune into a TV show to see how a story plays out. We can fast-forward to find out if the good guy got the girl, who won in the end, or if the truth came out. Think about doing this in real life. If you could fast-forward to determine the outcomes of your actions, what would you like to know? What would your followers like to know?

Effective leaders learn to fast-forward by developing a vision of what they want to see in the future. You probably have done this many times on the way to initiating new ways of doing business. However, whether you jump ahead to this new reality intuitively or move methodically, you need to bring other people along with you by "playing out the tape" for them. When possible, actually show people your thinking, with flowcharts and other images, to help them see what you envision.

Beth, the leader of a family-owned firm, realized that the employee benefits system was costing her retail operation more and more money. Looking down the road, she could see that in two to three years the impact of the costs might sink the small organization. She discussed the needed changes with her HR manager and a consultant but did not share her thoughts with the company as a whole. When it was time to introduce the changes, it dawned on her that her employees might see the shift in a negative light. Beth decided to play out the tape as she saw it. She and her HR manager developed talking

When possible, actually show people your thinking, with flowcharts and other images, to help them see what you envision.

points to take her team through the challenge, options, and desired solution(s). As she played out the tape for her team, they were able to embrace the changes and plan how to introduce them to the rest of the organization.

You might find that you and your team become uncomfortable with the difficult conversations you can envisage as you discuss the alternative options in the "tape." Once you've gone through the tape with your staff, you need to help them prepare their staff too. For those unaccustomed to or uncomfortable with explaining things, you may need to assign a partner to help them through the initial phase.

No matter how much time it takes, it's worth a lot of communication effort to play out the tape so that you lead employees in their time frame and not yours. They need to be privy to data or other learning that helped you come to your conclusions. Perhaps as the leader you have thought about the changes for a while. When you have them all straight in your mind, you start to think that your followers do too. You may think that everyone else will quickly "get" what's needed and embrace your thinking. However, they haven't had the privilege of thinking it all through over time the way you have. You may have come to your strategy as the result of an intuitive leap in thinking, but other people may need a more step-by-step approach to help them see the entire tape. If you don't play out the tape before and after your realizations, you may encounter resistance to organizational change and to your vision. Leaders often take the resistance personally or get impatient. But others need to see the whole tape to buy in. Play it out for them.

TRUTH 20

LEADERS FRAME THE DISCUSSION

The training manager saw the new leadership development program as a great opportunity to help staff with the tricky transition from individual contributor to leadership, meeting identified learning needs. He was disappointed when the executive team failed to approve it. They, in contrast, saw the program as a costly substitute for coaching by each leader's boss, and they didn't want to spend extra money without good reason.

So the manager rewrote his proposal, renaming it the "Adding Value Through Leadership" initiative. Although the content remained unchanged, this time he stressed the increased efficiency and income that more-confident and dynamic leaders would bring. And you know what? When it next came before the executive committee, they approved it right away.

How you describe something has a tremendous impact on how others understand it. You may think that facts are facts, and that if something is clear to you it will be clear to everyone. However, the reality is that how people see things varies enormously, depending on their past experiences, their position in the organization, and their view of how the world works.

How people see things varies enormously, depending on their past experiences, their position in the organization, and their view of how the world works.

As a leader, it's vital that you learn how to articulate or "frame" your thinking in a way that anticipates perceived needs and shapes others' responses to your advantage. Just like the frame around a picture, a good verbal frame draws attention to its contents in a certain way, affecting how they are perceived. When you choose a powerful frame, capturing others' imaginations with your choice of words, they are more likely to see the discussion through your eyes.

Linguist George Lakoff has shown how politicians use framing to set the terms of the debate. Right-wing politicians, for instance, replaced the idea of "tax cuts" or "reduction" with that of "relief." Since the word relief is associated with getting rid of pain, the concept of taxes is thus positioned as something from which you suffer, and from which the good guys provide relief. With repetition, the new phrase becomes the normal one to use, reinforcing the message. Once the frame is accepted as the norm, it becomes very hard for anyone else to position taxes as something that should go up, since that would mean taking away the relief.

Let's look at another organizational example. Daniel, head of a major design firm, had problems with staff not communicating effectively beyond division boundaries. They didn't understand that they needed to commit not just to their part of the organization, but at a regional level too. When Daniel started describing the organization as "one big family," in which members supported their brothers and sisters on a daily basis but sometimes also had to think about the needs of distant cousins, his employees began to "get it." Daniel reinforced the message by making his team aware of how many perks they received in vacation time, nights out, and deep-pocket healthcare by working for such a family-oriented firm.

Clever leaders ensure that their frames are well received by taking time to prepare and practice them before any important occasion. They also do the following:

1. **Keep it simple.** A successful frame is simple and clear enough for everyone to understand and remember. The clearer you are with your messages, the better your followers will see what you stand for.

2. **Keep saying it.** The more you share your leadership message with others, and the more consistent it is, the more likely it is that those others will take in your message and act on it.

3. **Keep it real.** Although it's important to present your ideas in a positive and future-oriented way, you should always be truthful and acknowledge gaps between your frame and reality. Make it clear that your frame is about a long-term vision that you are working to achieve.

Consciously or not, you are constantly applying frames to your leadership messages through the language you use. So make your words powerful and effective through the judicious use of framing.

PART V

THE TRUTH ABOUT LEADERSHIP PRESENCE AND POWER

TRUTH 21

A LEADER IS ALWAYS "ON"

Actors about to go onstage have their dressing rooms. Stars preparing to appear on a talk show wait in a place called the "green room," composing themselves for their performance. It's amazing to watch the transformation when they walk onto the set. They turn on like a light as they become their characters or assume their public personae. Their high energy generates a mood that captures the audience.

Good leaders do the same thing when appearing in front of an audience, using their words, facial expressions, and even bodies to convey that they are in control, inspired, and in a positive frame of mind. However, when you are a leader, your audience is an all-day one—every follower, contact, and client with whom you work, right down to your company driver. Highly visible, you set the tone for your team or organization. Others take their lead from you, looking for reassurance that everything is on course, and for encouragement to drive things forward. Tempting as it may be, you can't slip out of your leader role until you are alone in your office, home, or hotel room.

What do we mean by the leader role? What traits or characteristics do you need to display? Well, by the time you reach leadership level, others will expect maturity in approach and thoughtfulness in outlook from you, as well as a positive belief in your organization or team and its capabilities. This means always projecting a can-do attitude and doing your best not to show anger or disappointment, no matter how challenging the situation.

This scenario is an ideal. Although you should work toward it, you are human. You will have moments of doubt, uncertainty, or negativity when problems occur and events take a troubling turn. Being "on" certainly doesn't mean that you always feel positive. But you manage your negativity. Once you're in your office, offstage, behind closed doors, you can heave a sigh or punch a cushion or two. But then you need to be able to put your negativity aside and think about the way forward. The longer you spend thinking about what went wrong or who did what wrong, the less you will look at solutions.

> *Being "on" certainly doesn't mean that you always feel positive. But you manage your negativity.*

Being "on" is not about denying that there are problems. Nor is it about deceiving people. It's about ensuring that your staff works in an environment that's as secure and positive as possible to keep them focused, energized, and on-task. This means that when times are tough, maintaining your positive leader role is more important than ever. However, this role needs to be delivered with clarity and honesty. Once a business problem occurs, present the facts as soon as possible to those who need to know—those who may feel the consequences—but just the facts, free of emotion and fear. Before you present them, make sure that you've taken the time to compose yourself and to think about some possible steps forward. That way, the overall agenda is presented as a challenge, not a problem or disaster, steering people toward thinking and working their way back to firmer ground.

Your apparent state of mind has a major impact on your staff and teammates. Slipping out of role not only affects their faith in your current strategy or the business as a whole, but it also affects their attitude toward you. Public moments of anger or sarcasm toward staff, or doubt, negativity, or panic about business initiatives can weaken people's confidence in your ability to keep the organizational ship on course. You will have forever changed in the eyes of your audience. It's a bit like seeing Santa Claus curse; once the mask has fallen, however briefly, it's almost impossible for the magic to return.

TRUTH 22

CHOOSE YOUR BATTLES CAREFULLY

When one of Katherine's direct reports was criticized in a partner's meeting, she was tempted to defend him, but she hesitated. She had put great effort into gaining the goodwill of the partner who was displeased with her subordinate, and defending him would cost her significant political capital, especially if her employee turned out to be in the wrong.

So Katherine waited to get the facts before jumping in. She was aware that political capital is like a bank account: You add to your account when you support others and are successful, and you make withdrawals when you oppose others or upset them.

When the people around you are happy with how you treat them, your political capital accounts are healthy, but when you strain or test your relationships, those accounts gradually empty. These are long-term investments, not quid pro quo (something for something) arrangements. You may make innumerable goodwill deposits with someone before you need to make a withdrawal. You'll find that your account with that person grows over time.

Wise leaders keep all their accounts in the black, not just the ones with their colleagues and superiors. Every time you go to bat for one of your team members, you add to that political capital account. When you demand a quick turnaround or extra effort, you make a withdrawal.

Giving a colleague a heads-up that keeps him or her out of trouble could buy you significant political capital.

You can gain political capital every day by showing real interest in others' contributions—listening to them, supporting them, and even simply saying thank you. You can also boost your political capital by socializing with people and casually keeping them in the know about things that may affect their work.

The size of a political capital deposit or withdrawal depends on how important the information or interaction is to the other person. Giving a colleague a heads-up that keeps him or her out of trouble could buy you significant political capital. Taking the blame for a superior's mistake could even earn you enough for a promotion or a plum assignment. But be sure to consider the long-term consequences on your accounts with others before you make such a large deposit with one person.

Withdrawals from your accounts also vary in size, depending on how much the issue matters to the people involved. Making someone look bad in front of others can result in a very large withdrawal, but some people are more sensitive than others. For some, any questioning or push back will result in a withdrawal, but other people see that kind of give-and-take as routine or even desirable. Take your cue from the other person and tread carefully until you can predict how he or she is likely to interpret your actions.

Also take extra care when you are under stress: A scrupulously maintained account can be quickly emptied by just a few short words or angry reactions. In the heat of the moment you may not even realize that you are behaving inappropriately, but others will.

Katherine kept her cool and later found that there was some merit to her colleague's complaint. So she talked privately with both her colleague and her employee, which added to her political capital with each of them.

TRUTH 23

YOUR STRESS RIPPLES ACROSS THE ORGANIZATION

At the end of a long, hard day, have you ever shocked yourself by lashing out at someone who didn't deserve it? Do you become impatient with small errors or slips of the tongue? If someone misspeaks and says "Saturday night" instead of "Friday night," do you get annoyed? If so, you're probably suffering from the "spillover effect."

Psychologist Fritz Perls coined this term to describe what happens when people become overwhelmed by stress. Physical and emotional tension fills us like water in a cup, or trash in a wastebasket, until eventually it overflows and affects those around us. If we use the trash can analogy, you've thrown old bits of anger and resentment into the basket and tried to ignore them. The trash can contains critical comments you received recently and even some from your childhood. It has accumulated all of kinds of physical stressors, like your flu symptoms, your lack of sleep, and the hangover you're nursing. When the old stuff spills over, it "smells" stronger from being stuffed in the trash can for so long.

Stress is a term that everyone bandies about at some time. Everyone is always stressed, and everything is stressful in today's workplace. But what do we actually mean by it? We mean anything that adds to what we have to do each day that upsets our minds and bodies. Since there are lots of these annoyances in our everyday world, they do add up. When you add the slings and arrows of our earlier lives, the stressors are quite a mix.

While stress can cause problems for people at any level of an organization, as a leader, your spillover affects your staff and colleagues every day. Your abrasive attitude or your condescending way of speaking can sap your group's energy, creating anxiety, depression, and conflict. When your stress spills over, your staff may think that you don't like their ideas or may be afraid to run things by you because of your harsh reactions. Your colleagues may not think of you as a team player because you can be abrasive when you speak with them.

Yaakov spent his younger years in the Israeli military. He developed quick reflexes and learned to "take no prisoners" in how he dealt with people. With his business leadership role in a multinational company, he got things done in the same "no holds barred" way. If there was a deal to make, he would go after it. His peers and subordinates saw him as inconsiderate in how he rolled over them when he felt it was needed. He didn't give them "breathing room" so that they could do their best; he wanted to make things happen in his time frame. His stress made him a terrible delegator because he was so impatient.

Yaakov was familiar with the feeling of being in the middle of a police action. He recognized the tightening of the muscles in his neck, chest, and thighs. Part of the familiar feeling was having trouble breathing and finding that he was breathing shallowly. His heart would beat fast. When he felt this way he knew that he would react fast to ensure the safety of his troops. But now that he was no longer in the military, he had learned how to breathe deeply and relax his thighs and neck muscles. His relaxation techniques worked best when he had time to use them before the tension got to be too much. So he knew that he had to take

Physical and emotional tension fills us like water in a cup, or trash in a wastebasket, until eventually it overflows and affects those around us.

some time when he felt the tension mounting in his body. If not, it would transfer to his reactions.

Of course, the best thing to do is to keep the trash can from filling up in the first place. You can do a number of things to keep your "trash," or stress, level down. They are the **practical physical things that really make a difference:**

- **Eat, drink, and rest regularly.** Drink plenty of water. When hungry, snack on protein foods such as meat, fish, hard-boiled eggs, nuts, and protein bars (not energy bars, which are high in sugar). Caffeinated drinks and sugary snacks may give you a temporary boost but can also make you agitated and cause mood slumps and even depression. Take catnaps whenever you can.

■ **Reduce muscle tension.** When your muscles are tense, your attitude gets rigid too. To keep them loose, exercise when you can, taking stretch and walk breaks; tense and relax your muscles, starting with your face and moving to your toes; and breathe deeply, focusing your eyes in the distance.

You also can take steps that will help **reduce your group's stress**:

■ **Factor stress into timelines.** Deadline pressure magnifies even the smallest stresses. When you schedule completion dates, give yourself and others a cushion of time to handle small delays and setbacks.

■ **Delegate and empower.** Think of what you do as not just making money or delivering services but also enabling others to do their jobs well. That includes clearly delegating responsibilities and trusting others to carry them out and to let you know how they're doing. You'll find that requesting follow-up will relieve your stress.

It's your job to keep yourself mentally and physically in shape so that you can keep your cool and lower your stress levels each day.

TRUTH 24

LET YOUR ENERGY BE LIKE FINE CHAMPAGNE—NOT TOO BUBBLY OR FLAT

When the new leader walked into the room, he had a twinkle in his eye and an upbeat message about where the organization was going. His calm yet bubbly manner was both soothing and invigorating. When he smiled, his dimples gave him a jolly look. By the time the meeting was over, his new followers were aligned with his preliminary views about moving forward and were ready to be reengaged in their work.

Like a glass of fine champagne, a leader's manner should be just energetic enough to be pleasantly stimulating. His or her effervescent manner should align people the way that bubbles line up in champagne. With too little fizz, you come across as flat and boring. But at the other extreme—being overcarbonated, like a shaken can of soda—you risk overwhelming people. When you consciously calibrate your level of energy, or carbonation, you will leave those around you feeling energized and engaged.

Your fizz, or energy, has an impact on everyone around you. Sophie found that when she was passionate about her leadership message, some of her followers thought she was "shouting" and were confused by what they thought were the hidden messages in her overcarbonation. On the other hand, Ian found that when he felt committed, other people wondered where he stood, because his manner and tone of voice tended to stay flat. Others said that he was "hard to read." Both Sophie and Ian wanted their followers to know where they stood and where the organization was going. For different reasons, their messages were hard to interpret.

People respond to the strength of your energy, so they can be overwhelmed by strong positive reactions, just as they are by strong negative ones. They confuse the two because they experience the strength of the energy the same way. Even if your intention is to be encouraging, if you are too forcefully positive, those around you may react in a defensive or even aggressive way. A leader needs to show his or her passion and commitment. But when does passion become "pushy?" In a society where animated and enthusiastic speaking is the norm, approaching your listeners that way encourages them to return the favor, but where it's not, it could be a big mistake. The dividing line is often cultural. What may come across as passionately optimistic in New York may seem like over-the-top evangelism in London.

There are several ways to keep your energy effervescent rather than flat or overcarbonated:

- At a basic level, you need to pay attention to your health and well-being by keeping your caffeine and sugar intake low and exercising or taking walks that relax overcarbonated energy and rev up flat energy.
- Use the time before you have to speak with other people to relax and prepare.

- Know when you will find it hard to be effervescent because of personal or business stress, and postpone or pay extra attention to your energy impact.

- Frame what you are saying by indicating that you are passionate and committed to overcoming flat energy and to explaining the reason for overcarbonated energy.

Having the right energy level is especially important when your team or colleagues are under the gun with time pressure. Before you dig in your heels and demand top performance, step back and consider how you're delivering your message. Do you seem overcarbonated in your eagerness to get things done? This is not about "emotional intelligence" but about the sheer impact of your energy on others. If the energy you're putting forth is at a level that's palatable to your team, it's fine. But how do you determine if your energy is palatable and, indeed, energizing for them? You, or someone you trust, can observe your audience's facial and body reactions, whether it's a large group, a few people, or just one person. You can always ask for feedback. Depending on individuals' preferences, there will be variations. Early on in your leadership tenure, others will grant you a lot of goodwill. Use that time to calibrate the energy that you put out, and compromise and find alternative ways of getting your message across.

TRUTH 25

YOU NEED TO "READ" LIKE A LEADER IN THE BLINK OF AN EYE

W hat people see in front of them is powerful. Marketers know this. They pick their actors and spokespeople to "read" right—to look and feel believable in the blink of an eye—for their products. Young, hip actors sell soft drinks better, and substantial middle-aged businesspeople capably represent their own companies. The viewers don't notice every nuance of the person's behavior or look, but they do notice how the person reads overall. If that character is credible, the viewer is more likely to believe in the product.

This message has strong implications for the workplace. As a leader, however well you speak, or however intelligent your words, you still need to "read" as a leader if you are to have the impact you want. Why? Your overall body language has the greatest impact on others—perhaps 60% of what they remember about you—since most people notice visual clues first and retain them longest. Next comes your tone of voice, making up perhaps 30% of what people remember. The least remembered is usually the content of what you say: about 10% of the impact. This means that, in key meetings and presentations, you need to present yourself as a leader with every part of yourself that's visible to others.

If you want to read like a leader every time you communicate, observe the following pointers:

> *Leaders tend to look neutral to positive except in very serious moments.*

- **Set your intention.** Your mind-set is a powerful force for grounding you and putting you in a leadership frame of mind. If you think ahead about what you want to accomplish, you'll make a team meeting or presentation more powerful and effective. Do you want to move people to action? Empower them? When you move up in an organization, how you set your thinking subtly affects how you react to others. And your team gets it! Like children with their parents, it's amazing how soon your team learns to read you and your thinking by how you set your face and position your body. They will interpret every shrug, frown, and clench of your teeth. Since you can't control all your expressions and movements, you should prepare your body to know how you want to come across by preparing your thinking instead. You might prethink: "In this meeting I will come across as in control of the situation and optimistic about the outcomes of this challenge."

- **Compose your expression.** Is this a serious communication or a motivational one? Carefully set your expression to match the mood. Look in a mirror, or ask a colleague to give you feedback on how your expression comes across. If you are uncomfortable about setting your expression, remember that leaders tend to look neutral to positive except in very serious moments. Here's a tip: Use your smile judiciously on an occasional basis, or smile with your eyes only. Even president Jimmy Carter lost impact with his trademark toothy smile.

■ **Compose your hands.** Whether standing in front of an audience or sitting at a conference table, hold your hands in front of you in the "steeple," or a kind of relaxed prayer position, with your fingertips touching. This is the classic hand position for leaders worldwide. Holding your hands this way helps you control unwanted gestures or nervous habits like pulling your hair or clutching the arms of your chair. The "point" of the steeple invades the space in front of you, especially when you're sitting at a table, and therefore gives the unconscious message that you are in charge because you're claiming the space.

To see how successful leaders "read," make it your business to observe how they present themselves on television. BBC's *Breakfast with David Frost*, CNN's *Last Word* and *Lou Dobbs Tonight*, and ABC's *Good Morning America* all regularly showcase world leaders. Try turning off the sound and just watching the picture to see how each of the leaders "reads" and what they do with their bodies, faces, and hands.

From Vladimir Putin, whose neutral-to-positive facial expression helped George W. Bush see him as trustworthy, to Tony Blair, with his relaxed and friendly open body posture, these leaders have practiced composing themselves to read right for their roles. You need to practice too. It's worth taking time to pay attention to your look and feel if you want to fulfill your leadership role and potential.

TRUTH 26

GOOD LEADERSHIP IS THE WISE USE OF POWER

Niccolo Machiavelli is infamous for writing "Power corrupts, and absolute power corrupts absolutely." His observations of the 16th-century Italian Medici court helped him truly understand how often power is misused. Yet he also believed that, with the wise use of power, leaders can generate great visions that stir the souls of others.

You cannot ignore the issue of power as a leader. On a basic level, you simply have it, because you get to make decisions and influence outcomes for others. That is not inherently a good or bad thing, just a fact. The real issue is how you put that power to use. People often think of power in negative terms because it is easy to abuse. Being in charge certainly requires you to take control. The key, however, is to do so with benign or positive intent toward your followers, rather than narcissistic self-interest.

Some people love the idea of power and jump to take charge. Others are more reluctant to flex their muscles. What we all have in common is the duty to learn to use power wisely, balancing any natural tendencies to overuse it or underuse it. Used to maximum effect, your leadership power will *empower* your organization and its employees. Used carelessly, it will *disempower* them by making them wait for you to make decisions or by creating fear of disapproval.

You'll know how you are using the power available to you by observing your own behavior and getting feedback from others. Use the following chart to help you think about this. Ask yourself which column you fall into for each issue. Be honest! Then ask yourself if that is who you want to be as a leader. If you don't like what you see on the chart, start thinking about what you need to do to change. That self-awareness is the first step to becoming a wise leader.

Underuse of Power	Wise Use of Power	Abuse of Power
Wants someone else to make decisions	Enjoys taking control to ensure the best results but will let others take the lead when they can	Wants to make all decisions and have the last word
Moves at own speed, not checking with others	Influences others	Vetoes others' decisions
Won't set specific expectations or standards	Creates consistency and standards	Demands perfection as the only option
Hates politics; avoids dealing with conflict	Uses politics and relationships to support ideas	Manipulates politics to drive own agenda

People who underuse their power tend to want someone else to make decisions, they move at their own measured or slow speed without consulting others, and they hate to

Although you may have basic power automatically through your title, true power can only be bestowed on you by the people you lead.

"play politics." In relation to their followers, they may be reluctant to set expectations and deadlines, give tough feedback, or move people out when they're not right for a role.

Abuse of power occurs when a leader demands constant recognition, perfection, and work done his or her way. Abuse gets even easier to recognize when leaders use power to demand special perks for themselves.

For the wise and moderate use of power, you need to set high but reachable goals and enjoy being in charge and influencing others. It's even better when you use your power to set broad organizational goals that you then translate into specific actions. It's also useful to put in place some consistency and standards that help you sort out organizational politics, since that will lead to fewer special favors.

The good of the organization should always be at the heart of what you do. For some people, this means speaking up and pushing people in a way that goes against their nature. For others, it means subduing their natural urge to just take charge and pull others in their wake. Finding the right balance ensures that employees feel secure and cared for as they rise to the challenges of organizational life.

Although you may have basic power automatically through your title, true power can only be bestowed on you by the people you lead. Real power comes from your staff believing in your expertise and trusting you as a leader while knowing that you have the clout to get things done on their behalf. This makes them want to follow you. In a virtuous circle, the more people want to follow you, the more power you have.

No matter what kind of organization you lead, it's how you use power that distinguishes your leadership tenure.

PART VI

THE TRUTH ABOUT
GETTING THINGS
DONE

TRUTH 27

OFTEN THE BEST DECISION IS EMPOWERING SOMEONE ELSE TO DECIDE

In his farewell address to the American people, President Harry Truman referred to his favorite motto, "The buck stops here," when he said, "The President—whoever he is—has to decide. He can't pass the buck to anybody. No one else can do the deciding for him. That's his job."

It's your job to ensure that the right decisions are made in your organization. But who makes them is another matter. Although you are ultimately responsible for all of them, you simply can't make every decision yourself. It's also not in your best interest to do so. You probably have more experience than the others, and you're less likely to make mistakes. But you got that experience by making decisions. Your team can develop the same way if you carefully choose times to let them make a decision. Experienced leaders know that delegating some decisions is vital to the development of their teams.

Of course, allowing others to make decisions can be unnerving. New leaders are often confused when followers don't make the same choices they would make. When someone makes the "wrong" decision, inexperienced leaders want to jump in and take over by making the "right" one. They're scared that they will lose control of the project, initiative, or campaign.

Good decision-making, therefore, is about finding a safe balance. The expected consequences of a decision, as well as the potential unexpected consequences, should determine who makes it. Some decisions you need to make yourself, and others are best left to your team or made with them.

Your decision-making options include the following:

- **The leader alone.** The leader makes the decision alone during a pressing emergency or when there is little time to involve others. This is a less-than-optimum solution that you should use only when necessary.

- **The leader with input from your team.** The act of giving input can be a learning experience for your team. Many important and urgent decisions, such as a "go/no go" on a project or investing in a new company or product, also require input from others, such as experts, other leaders, and partners.

- **The leader in equal partnership with your team.** These decision-making moments are often learning opportunities for everyone involved. The process allows all relevant parties to have a productive dialogue and debate, which yields better decisions.

New leaders are often confused when followers don't make the same choices they would make.

- **Your team with input from you.** Assess the potential downside for mistakes, and balance that against the possible upside: a learning opportunity for your team. If a marketing campaign isn't quite perfect, or your team doesn't land the best local celebrity, how much of a problem would that be? Can you live with it in the name of their learning? You can also give them some coaching and guidance without telling them what to do.

- **Your team on their own.** If the cost won't be too severe in terms of time, quality, or money (there is always some cost to mistakes), you can let the decision go entirely.

As a leader, you have a number of roles with conflicting responsibilities. On the one hand, you are in charge of execution. On the other, your job is also to develop your subordinates. You can achieve both aims by empowering your employees to help you with the strategic development of your organization. People learn by making decisions—both good ones and poor ones. Look for opportunities to let them learn and grow.

TRUTH 28

ADJUST YOUR LEADERSHIP STYLE TO FIT THE EMPLOYEE

The 24-year old South Asian computer technician has good qualifications and speaks English well, so your company hires her to service an important computer system. You give her a cubicle and the tools of her trade, tell her to call you if she needs help, and go on a business trip. Because she is experienced—you paid top dollar for her through a head-hunter —and gung ho about the work, you think she can handle things. Unbeknownst to you, however, she is devastated. She thinks she's been abandoned, and, floundering in her task, she decides to quit after a week. What went wrong?

A job has several foundations: skills, experience, motivation, and supervision. The new employee had the first three but needed more supervision than expected. Frequently, someone new in a job or new to the company needs a **telling or parental style** of leadership, in which you or another designated lead person lets her know specifically what she needs to do and what your expectations are for parameters such as quality, time, and cost. In some parts of the world, such as South Asia and South America, employees may expect more personal treatment and may see it as a sign that you care.

If you can convince your computer techie to stay with the company, she likely will appreciate a telling style of leadership from you at first, but after 9 to 12 months, she may prefer a **coaching style**. In coaching her, you give feedback on how she is doing and what she can do to be even more effective. You will still need to do some telling at times, such as when she is dealing with a particularly difficult client or entering a new project area. A coaching style of leadership may be tiring, but by paying close attention to your employees, identifying alternatives for them, and encouraging them to try new things, you can help them become more independent and proficient in their roles.

At that point, your employees can make day-to-day decisions in the areas they know. Then, your job as a leader may be to use a **supporting style** to make sure that the right processes are in place and that you are there when your employees need some coaching or guidance. You may still take part in decisions and assist in setting the work agenda, goals, and objectives, but you won't do a lot of day-to-day hand-holding unless there's a problem at work or even in the employee's personal life. In your techie's case, she might not need your help in staying motivated, but she might need to know that you're around to give her a hand if needed and that you will be supportive if, for instance, her mother is ill.

There may come a moment when you can use a **delegating style** with your technician, once she gets to know the job inside and out. Many people on your team can negotiate their own agendas, goals, and objectives, so you can let go except for the times when they need your help. And at this point in their careers, they should be the ones to tell you when they need guidance.

So how do you know which leadership style a follower needs? It is easy to err in either direction: delegating too much too early, or being overly instructive. Unfortunately, it's often a mismatch between your style and your employee's needs that lets you know you're on the wrong track.

Consider another scenario: You're going on vacation, so you hand over work to an experienced member of your team. You lay out what needs to be done in a handover, or discussion, document. If you write extremely specific instructions, you will insult your subordinate. The key here is to talk it over so that everyone is clear about expectations and where to go for help. This is tricky, because some people may say that they can do it, but then they fall short. So it's best to test someone before you leave town by having him help you on some work to see how he does.

> *Your goal is not only to get work done, but also to preserve and build your rapport and relationship with your subordinates.*

Your goal is not only to get work done, but also to preserve and build your rapport and relationship with your subordinates. Telling and coaching, when junior employees need it, and supporting and delegating, when experienced followers are ready for it, are good ways to develop your team members.

TRUTH 29

No Good Deed Goes Unpunished

Everybody liked Charlie. A highly regarded senior manager, not only did he have far more experience than most of his colleagues, but he was a steady and thoughtful leader, open to and respectful of others' views. However, Charlie didn't like pushing his clients. He was also reluctant to demand performance from his team if there was any chance he might be perceived as aggressive. The result? Despite his ability, he got flak from his management and was known as a pushover. The last time I saw him, he was still waiting for a promotion.

As a leader, you don't need to be liked; you need to be respected. However much that advice may go against your nature, it's one of the most important points to remember when entering a leadership position. If you try too hard to be nice, not only will others likely look down on you or see you as a "soft touch," they may also take advantage of your good nature. This doesn't mean being mean or ruthless in your treatment of others. You just need to be careful about doing favors or letting people get away with even small things. Always play out the intended and unintended consequences of any "special" decisions regarding your staff. Good deeds can backfire.

"Good deeds" come in three varieties:

1. **Special favors or exceptions.** When you're a "nice guy," you understand that people have unexpected personal needs. You want to do the right thing by others and to trust their judgment. But when someone asks you for time off, to leave early, or to deliver late on an assignment, stop and think before you grant his or her request. Play out the worst-case consequences of your decision. For example, will others in your group feel shortchanged or resentful? Grant favors only if you feel you can explain to others why the case is a special one. Remember that when you grant favors to one individual too often, it's called favoritism.

> *As a leader, you don't need to be liked; you need to be respected.*

2. **Letting people off the hook.** It's your responsibility to demand the best from all members of your team and to push back when they push you. Once you allow someone to miss a deadline, nine times out of ten he or she will try to do the same thing again. Make your team aware that there are very few situations in which it's reasonable to renege on a commitment. When it comes to deadlines, they must give you good advance warning if they feel themselves getting into difficulties. That allows you to

work out a contingency plan with them. Only in cases of extreme emergency is a last-minute back-out acceptable.

3. **Doing for others what they can do for themselves.** Sometimes your staff needs to air their concerns with you. Sometimes that's fine. It's part of your role to help them learn. But not all the time. Make sure team members don't get too dependent on advice. Discourage them from coming straight to you with a question. Suggest that they check with others or experiment on their own first. And when they do come, ask them challenging questions that help them think through the problem for themselves, rather than just giving them an answer. You have to be cruel to be kind; pushing back in this way helps them develop as competent individual players.

When you establish clear boundaries, you'll get better performance from others, because they will figure out things for themselves. Consistently fair but firm leaders are respected and usually appreciated.

TRUTH 30

THE STRUCTURE IS NOT THE ORGANIZATION, JUST AS THE MAP IS NOT THE TERRITORY

There's an old story about a man looking for something under a streetlight. A passerby stops and asks what he's looking for. His keys, he says, and carries on. After a while the passerby asks where exactly the keys were lost. The man says it was down the block. So why is he looking under the streetlight? "That's where the light is."

In the intense search for better results, companies commonly look to restructuring exercises. Restructuring means changing organizational relationships and groupings or the way in which work is allocated and done. These days, in the face of tough global competition, restructuring is often done to cut costs and increase profits. It's a popular pastime because it's "where the light is": an easy exercise to do on paper—moving around boxes, titles, and roles on the organization chart. But just like our friend at the lamppost, many organizations aren't really looking in the right place. Those restructuring exercises, while making the organization "leaner" and, in many respects, "meaner," all too often don't make it any more effective.

The truth about restructuring is not "don't do it." In fact, the first truth of intelligent restructuring is that, in a healthy organization, it happens all the time. Good leaders keep a constant eye on organizational patterns and processes, making subtle changes—a better person for that job, a better way of delivering that project—one after the other, all the time. They don't just wait until they need a boost or have a problem. The second truth is that, unfortunately, no guaranteed formula for success exists. There are several ways to look at and structure organizations; all of them have their place. The third truth is that it's the soft stuff, like people, that counts, and much of this can't be seen or measured on a chart.

All too often restructuring exercises miss the point because they are too focused on what is happening on that piece of paper. They tend to look at the "hard" components of an organization, which can be easily pinned down in a diagram: structure, strategy, and systems. The diagram leads to logical outcomes, determining who might need to be moved and who might need to go. What this approach misses is that the "softer" elements of organizational life have an equal or greater impact on how an organization functions. These include **staff**, **skills**, and **shared values**. The quality and nature of all of these require careful consideration when you're making changes.

If you do decide to go in for a major organizational redesign, it pays to choose a soft or people-led approach. Rather than looking only at the figures, consider how any proposed changes will play out with your workforce. Will lean staffing make for more irritable and uncompromising leaders who will step on people's toes? Perhaps the skills you already have represented in that workforce might suggest ways of tackling a problem that don't involve reducing head count. If the organization's shared values will be affected by the changes, consider that however much sense they make economically, the fallout in terms of lost motivation may have a stronger negative impact. Many sports teams have found that trading respected players costs them the winning chemistry they developed over time. You have likely invested considerably in your employees' training, loyalty, and organizational knowledge. It pays to weigh your employees' needs against the pennies you might save in the short term. You don't want to waste your investment.

> *Many sports teams have found that trading respected players costs them the winning chemistry they developed over time.*

As the leader of an organization, before you effect change, be sure to balance present needs against the long-term potential of the skills you have in place. Ideally, rather than impose abrupt change, you'll gently readjust your organizational structure to reflect how your skills base is developing, or how you want it to develop in years to come, in an ongoing manner. If you want young players to develop leadership ability, for instance, it's worth creating small units where they can learn more complex skills progressively. With a bit of luck, and a lot of application, by keeping your eye on the ball with the small changes that make sense, you'll avoid the need for painful and comprehensive restructuring further down the road.

TRUTH 31

COMING IN FROM THE OUTSIDE?
PAY YOUR DUES!

What would you do to succeed in a new leadership position? How far would you go to show that you care about your new organization? Would you roll up your sleeves, get down on your knees, and clean the staff toilets? That's not as extreme as it might sound. The leader in this chapter did just that in real life!

When Casey, new director of a state energy commission, stepped into the role, she faced several obstacles: she hadn't risen through the usual government ranks, her background was in local community projects, she lacked energy industry experience, and she was the first woman in the job. Not only that, but major organizational change was clearly required. Securing the job may have been a challenge, but keeping and delivering it looked tougher still. The bureaucrats figured she'd last two years at the most. Twelve years later, however, she was still there, ready for a more responsible position, and with a successor trained. During that time, her commission had been voted the nation's most effective, and she had been tapped by the government to lead the federal energy commission.

What Casey's new colleagues didn't realize was that her "irrelevant" background had given her great experience in creating partnerships and in getting diverse people on board. Casey knew that, before making changes, she needed to build credibility by showing employees at all levels that she cared about what they were doing. She also knew that it takes a long time not only to convince an organization that it needs to change, but to really embed that change. Above all, Casey understood that she had to pay her dues and, putting personal glory to one side, she was committed to doing so.

It takes a long time not only to convince an organization that it needs to change, but to really embed that change.

What advice would Casey give to other outsiders taking over a leadership position, especially when change is required?

- **Connect with people in person and by phone, not just through e-mail.** This is vital if you are to establish the relationships you'll later need to rely on when seeking support for changes. Casey spent her first two years visiting all 155 of the commission's sites. She showed up with her hard hat and steel-toed shoes and literally got her feet wet when she donned waders to check on the replacement of an ancient dam. In one remote location she chipped in and cleaned those famous toilets.

- **Get the "champions" on your side.** Spend time getting to know those people who really believe in and do sterling work on behalf of the organization. Once they believe in you, they will help you spread the new thinking across the organization in what they do and say. Casey got her champions noticed in state newspapers for their good work. She then could rally support from key decision-makers when she needed it. This encouraged others to follow suit.

- **Think holistically: don't change procedures in one place without looking at the impact elsewhere.** A "good deed" can get you in trouble. Casey found that when she let one location ignore a rule because of "special circumstances," other locations thought they could ignore the rules too. She finally decided that outside of natural disasters, there were no "special circumstances." Her consistency of treatment for all locations helped give her the reputation of being a firm and fair leader.

- **Involve people outside your organization.** Too many organizations get so inwardly focused that they lose touch with the needs of their customers. Casey understood the necessity, particularly for a state organization, of building civic engagement and of being open to questions and challenges from the outside world. When she established a "supporters of energy" group, her staff was initially annoyed. They saw it as busywork. However, when a series of rolling blackouts brought out angry community groups in force, the supporters group jumped in to assist with the crisis and ensure that electricity stayed available.

It took four years for Casey to get cultural change started and another eight years, and a crisis, for it to really take hold. Now, looking back, her commission is pleased with what they have achieved. They are particularly proud of the public involvement from all kinds of people—school kids to big companies. Casey's patience paid off.

TRUTH 32

DELEGATION IS A CONFIDENCE GAME

Joan joined a midsize consumer goods company to accelerate her career progression to management. With plenty of experience in fast-moving consumer goods, she immediately drew up a program of work for her team of three, quickly running it by them before getting the go-ahead from management. Then she jumped into the program with gusto, determined to prove herself.

To her surprise and disappointment, her team couldn't keep up with her. Delays and mistakes became common. Joan felt increasingly uncomfortable with how the others did things. She frequently jumped in to try to fix tricky situations, working frantically through evenings and weekends to keep up with the program. The result? She was exhausted, and her staff felt out of the loop.

Joan's story is a common one. She fell into a trap all too typical of great individual performers. With a tendency to deliver and achieve high results no matter what, she thought if she just gave her staff the work, they'd do it the same way she would. When they didn't, she was perplexed. Supremely confident in her marketing knowledge and experience, she nevertheless didn't have a clue about how to use her team.

What Joan had to learn is that successful delegation requires two interdependent yet separate types of confidence:

1. **Personal confidence** to let go and trust someone else to do the work, however much you believe you might be able to do it better.

2. **Leadership confidence** in your team's capacity to deliver the required results.

The first is about a state of mind, and Joan certainly didn't lack this. Willing to let go of her own attachment to the outcome, and to allow her staff to do things their way, she quickly gave her team lots of responsibility.

> *Confidence in your team should be based on more than just optimism. It needs to be firmly grounded in evidence.*

However, Joan fell at the second hurdle. Confidence in your team should be based on more than just optimism. It needs to be firmly grounded in evidence. As a leader, you need to strive to understand how your team works and then delegate to them accordingly, regularly checking on their progress.

A useful way of developing well-founded confidence

in your team is to consider their abilities and commitment, or **skills** and **wills**. If you take the time to test and observe team members, working out their individual levels of skill and will, you then can delegate more confidently, allocating tasks that match each person's potential.

Skill is a combination of experience, training, and a set of instinctive responses acquired through trial and error. Have your people learned what questions need to be asked or routes explored to complete a task? You can gain a sense of individuals' skills by looking at their work experience or feedback reports, as well as asking questions before starting a task. For instance, to vet, or test, how someone will work with a subcontractor, ask the person what questions he or she will ask the agency staff and how he or she will monitor progress.

Will is about commitment, determination, and what might be called "fire in the belly." In gaining a sense of people's will, you're looking not for heroics, but for a sense of urgency and enthusiasm when carrying out tasks and a willingness to ask for guidance when required.

When you're managing different skill-and-will combinations, the following principles are useful:

- **Low-skill, high-will** employees work well when apprenticed to someone else who has honed his or her instincts. They often respond well to training.

- **Low-will, high-skill** people often require some incentive to deliver. Ask what has motivated them during other projects—status, money, challenge, praise?

- **Low-skill, low-will** staff require you to consider whether this person is the wrong fit for your team or whether she is just discouraged. If it's the latter, you can look for ways in which to boost her self-esteem.

- **High-skill, high-will** people can be delegated to with confidence. You've hit pay dirt!

Building the confidence to delegate takes time. When you start a new position, don't rush into trying to deliver; take time to get to know your team and to build a work plan around their abilities rather than imposing one on them. Testing your team on smaller projects helps you build both your confidence in them and their confidence in themselves.

PART VII

THE TRUTH ABOUT MOTIVATING AND INSPIRING YOUR TEAM

TRUTH 33

QUESTIONS UNITE; ANSWERS DIVIDE

Questions are powerful things. While statements or facts set out a piece of information as it is, with little room for discussion, questions have the core purpose of seeking information. In an organizational context, questions, used wisely and with good intent, are about a collective quest for knowledge and insight, opening issues, drawing contributions, and generating dialogue.

A questioning perspective is essential to any leader who wants to build a strong team. Thoughtful leaders ask questions even before they start their jobs and keep asking them to stay in tune with others. They know that asking for opinions, listening to the answers, and then acting on them when appropriate not only gives them the power of many brains besides their own, however brilliant that is, but also makes those others feel valued and respected—part of a united team. In contrast, simply giving people the answers or the facts— telling them what to do—limits the possibility of fruitful discussion and disempowers people from thinking for themselves. It can even make others feel resentful and harden their position against you.

Asking questions is different from indecision. Indecision can frighten people, and as a good leader, you should not put pressure on others to make decisions on your behalf. But you should strive to make, and take pride in making, decisions from an informed position, welcoming perspectives that you might not have found for yourself. To solicit the very best ideas and suggestions, it's worth making the effort to craft your leadership questions carefully.

The best questions are often open-ended. If people can give a quick-fire answer, they may not stop to really think about the answer. However, a question that asks them to give a considered personal response encourages them to contribute. Once someone has contributed to a strategy or plan, it becomes easier to draw him or her into the delivery of that idea. That person now has a stake in the discussion and shares ownership of the possible outcomes with you and other contributors.

There are no "dumb" questions, but some are less unifying than others. "Why" questions can be tough for your people to answer. If someone says, "I think we should invest less in staff development this year," don't demand "Why?" People often don't know why something is so or should be so; they just have a hunch that their suggestion might be the right one. The directness of a "why" question can come across as somewhat aggressive, making people react defensively or freeze up. Instead, ask "What do you hope we could accomplish by that?" or "What would be the best and worst possible outcomes of that move?" You'll get where you want to go, but in a more gentle and productive way.

It's also important that you ask any questions in a spirit of curiosity and openness. Beware of statements disguised as questions, where you already know what you think the answer should be, or you want people to respond to you in a certain way. You have to be genuine in your questioning, not directive or manipulative. When you are looking for compliance with your answers, you lose the personal commitment of others and become an "answering" leader despite your superficial attempt to involve others.

> *Beware of statements disguised as questions, where you already know what you think the answer should be, or you want people to respond to you in a certain way.*

It's all too easy to become an "answering" leader without meaning to. Often people will ask you for an answer or ask how you want them to do something. Unless it is an emergency, try to pull back and encourage people to explore the options with you. As a leader, you create connections with others when you find questions that open their floodgates of ideas.

TRUTH 34

FEEDBACK IS THE BEST KIND OF CRITICISM

Great sports coaches know that you can push athletes hard if you do it to take them to the next level. People can do amazing things when you really need them to stretch to get work done quickly or to cover for others. Setting "stretch goals" can be exciting and inspirational. Ask people who worked in Silicon Valley start-ups in the early days. They loved every minute of not sleeping, along with the ecstasy of being part of something exciting and new.

But there's a dark side to "stretch goals." People can get burned out or worn out and can feel as if they're always being criticized for not doing the near-impossible. Criticism is part of working life. We all have to get it and give it, whether officially through appraisals or informally from bosses on a daily basis. However, we welcome it to varying degrees. If you think about your own experiences of receiving criticism, the times when you took it best were probably occasions when someone appeared to have your best interests at heart. You emerged from the discussion with a positive sense of what you needed to do next. This type of criticism is exemplified by the feedback that's part of good coaching.

You can help someone improve by encouraging him or her to see a situation objectively, rather than through the filter of a psychological assessment such as "You don't care about your colleagues' needs," which implies "good" and "bad." You achieve this by assuming a position of impartiality yourself, behaving not as a critic but as a neutral

> *It can be helpful to think of your eyes and ears as a television camera, objectively recording words and actions.*

observer. Describing current behavior in words that are free of anger and judgment allows you to steer people toward other ways of thinking or working without causing offense or resentment.

The first stage in delivering feedback is careful observation. Before saying anything, devote some time to thinking about how to describe a subordinate's behavior in a neutral way. It can be helpful to think of your eyes and ears as a television camera, objectively recording words and actions. Next, describe what you see to the person, offering a second picture of what might work better so that the gap between the current and improved behavior is evident. It's often helpful to give an example of a time when the person displayed the desired behavior. It brings a positive aspect to the criticism and shows that the person can change if he or she knows the way forward.

The final stage is to discuss together how to close that gap by creating a new picture. When talking to someone who tends to do things in a last-minute way, you might give an example like this one: "When you e-mail your presentation slides after everyone else, the meeting participants are annoyed and may complain to me and to each other." Then you can suggest ways to make sure that things are not done in a last-minute way by saying: "I've noticed that when your travel schedule forces you to finish a draft a week in advance, you let people you trust review it, which means that your work is beautifully done and on time." As the supervisor, you can encourage your employee to create an ongoing way to replicate his success strategy even when he's not forced to do so by circumstances.

The key to moving feedback into action is to find a way to duplicate or create successes. Although knowing what's wrong is a start, if you just tell people in the workplace to stop doing something, their instinctive reaction is either to defend what they're doing and continue as before or to focus so hard on not doing it that their behavior may appear uncomfortable or contrived. It's essential to find ways to encourage and reinforce positive change.

So, judiciously negotiate those stretch goals for each team member individually. Regularly give them the feedback they need to self-correct and keep going. When they succeed, celebrate with them from time to time. When they celebrate, it should feel like winning in Las Vegas so that they want to come back for more stretch goal challenges.

TRUTH 35

YOU HAVE MORE THAN
THE CARROT AND THE STICK

When the National Governors Association polled 10,000 high school students about their studies, it expected them to say they didn't want more work since school was pretty tough already. To their surprise, they found that students were disappointed that they weren't challenged enough! But, on reflection, is that so surprising? Although we may assume that most people would rather have an easy life than a difficult one, it goes without saying that we all also want our lives to have meaning. Activities at school and work are where many of us find that meaning as we discover, and play to, our strengths.

It's important as a leader that you find appropriate ways to challenge and stretch your staff on that journey of self-definition. That's not an easy task. Indeed, for many leaders, motivation is a bit of a mystery. Too often employees are seen as organizational mules, motivated only by offers of "carrots"— money or other perks—or threats of "sticks"—criticism or punishment. Although carrots and sticks work for all of us some of the time, motivation is actually far more complex than that.

As a leader, you are way ahead when you gain an understanding of what really drives people to do their best work. There's no quick-fix answer; what motivates one person does not always motivate another. But understanding the range of motivators helps you try different approaches on different people until you find those that work for you and your organization.

Carrots and sticks are both forms of extrinsic motivation. Extrinsic motivators are factors that come from outside of us, pushing us in a certain direction. Money, perks, and status symbols—the corner office, for example—are all obvious extrinsic motivators of the carrot variety. Praise is perhaps a less obvious one, along with its "stick" counterparts, criticism and humiliation.

These extrinsic tools are more prevalent in some professions than others—sales, for instance, with its bonus-linked salaries—and can work very well when used sparingly, as a mini-boost. They are easy motivators to offer because, although they can cost money, they require little real time and energy.

However, in most professions extrinsic motivators work less well in the long term. Although occasional carrots keep people hooked—something that the casinos of Las Vegas know well—if they occur too regularly the impact soon fades. People start to take the carrots for granted, and they become meaningless. Worse, overuse of extrinsic motivators can actually demotivate people

There's no quick-fix answer; what motivates one person does not always motivate another.

by setting up an unhealthy expectation. If an employee is used to getting a regular bonus or compliment, and then you end the habit, he may feel let down or abandoned and lose the will to keep pushing on.

If you really want to motivate people, you need to think about intrinsic motivators too. These are motivators that reflect people's internal beliefs and values about their place in the world and the way the world works. An employee who believes in order and systems, for example, may be turned off by being thrown into a challenge with no clear parameters, but he will do his best work when offered a role with repetition, structure, and planning. Someone who loves innovation and creativity, in contrast, often enjoys being given a challenge that allows him to think inventively and to explore and showcase his creative talents. Someone who wants to do the right thing in the world may be drawn to nonprofit work.

Many of the world's major businesses have realized that some of the best young employees they recruit are attracted to altruistic opportunities as well as intellectual challenges and money. They offer opportunities such as volunteering in the community as a way for their employees to stay motivated as part of their regular duties.

Pay attention to how your team members react to their work and to the rewards and recognition they are offered. What perks them up? What brings them down? Explore these questions with them at review meetings. Keep both intrinsic and extrinsic motivators in mind, and use them judiciously. You can then motivate individual team members in the way that suits each one best.

TRUTH 36

QUICK COACHING KEEPS YOUR TEAM ON COURSE

In prizefights the trainers rush to their boxers' corners after each round. Besides words of encouragement and a refreshing drink, they give some just-in-time coaching and useful guidance. The trainer's job in those one-minute rest periods is to prime his boxer to keep moving and stay focused while avoiding jabs and direct hits. That's what you want to do for your team members.

Translate those 60-second intervals into "coaching-in-action" minutes. These are brief coaching sessions with team members when they're in the midst of their work. What great timing to give them the sound bites they need to keep moving and stay out of harm's way. You can energize them with your confidence and conviction just when they need it. This is not only the time for quick kudos to buck people up. You can also provide constructive course corrections. Anything with a long-term trajectory needs guidance and feedback to stay on course and avoid obstacles, whether it's a guided missile or a strategy.

Before major presentations about long-term projects, the leader of one organization used to say, "This presentation could make or break your career. Don't screw it up." That was not very helpful, because his team members would freeze up. So he changed his coaching to give his team pointers such as "This executive really cares about cost projections. Be sure to go through that part of your presentation carefully." Or

It takes only a minute to rev up someone with a coaching moment.

"Focus on the people resources." Or "Stay away from Project X in your presentation; it's a hot button."

The executive learned the following:

1. Give team members rehearsal time with you before presentations to give them some quick coaching.

2. Don't correct unless it's vital for your team member's success.

3. Focus on the one or two things that will make a difference immediately.

4. Stay positive as you focus your team member on moving forward successfully.

It takes only a minute to rev up someone with a coaching moment. Just a few seconds of your time helps them stay in shape for what they need to do. As their coach, you need to do just that to develop winning players.

TRUTH 37

LITTLE THINGS MEAN A LOT

The great architect Mies van der Rohe famously said "God is in the details." He believed that it's not the grand designs that really matter so much as the supposedly unimportant details and the impact they have. A true craftsman, he paid attention to the design of his buildings, right down to the smallest element.

What is true in architecture can be true for life in general and certainly for life in the workplace. Although people are aware of the bigger picture and strive for success in it, it is often the apparently inconsequential details of organizational life—the reactions and remarks of leaders, for example—that they notice most, because these are the things that really affect their working experience. By paying attention to the small ways in which you communicate with others, you can add that extra value that makes people see their job as not just OK, but great. In return, they will show you commitment, positively affecting your leadership effectiveness. It takes only a few minutes each day to do those extra things that make the difference.

There are three main ways in which you can have an impact. Most of your followers will welcome being kept informed about what's happening, what's coming up, and how're they're doing. You may think, since you're aware of most everything, that others will be too, but this is not the case. You need to be explicit about your thoughts and observations. Good communication gives people the sense that management is paying attention to their activity and encourages them to buy into your plans. It doesn't have to be planned. In fact, it works best when it is simply on your radar screen all the time. You have loads of opportunities every day.

1. **What's happening.**

   Some things will always be confidential, and it's important to keep those quiet until you have the go-ahead. However, with those few exceptions, you should try to share as much as possible about the organization's projects and processes with your team, especially any good news. A weekly e-newsletter can be a good way to keep people in the know.

   Communication becomes even more important during times of uncertainty. Following Hurricane Katrina's onslaught in the U.S. South, caring leaders reassured employees by circulating information on staff well-being and assistance measures. Positive stories raise morale. Tell them, for instance, about the CFO who invited 37 survivors and their five dogs to his home!

2. **What's coming up.**

   This is a bit like "coming attractions." Your team will always appreciate a heads-up about upcoming new work or important events. For example, even if the details of an event are not finalized, you can still give people the guest list and draft agenda. If they will be put on the spot, make them aware of situations they may be placed in or questions they may be asked. "No surprises" is the guideline.

3. **How they're doing.**

Look for opportunities, private and public, to say good things about your team and to give them gentle pointers about what they're not doing so well and how to do it better. Most employees are eager to know how they're doing but don't want to ask. Regular informal conversations can be the best method. Stop by and talk to team members to connect with them personally. This high-touch approach—"management by walking around"—makes your employees feel they are seen as real people rather than cogs in the wheel.

Most employees are eager to know how they're doing but don't want to ask.

Others may say, "Don't sweat the small stuff." Although it's important to let go of perfectionism and refrain from obsessing about the details of the work, it is never a waste of time to pay attention to the little things that matter to other people anywhere in your life. Every little bit counts.

PART VIII

THE TRUTH ABOUT MOLDING YOUR TEAM

TRUTH 38

A LEADER CARES PASSIONATELY ABOUT DEVELOPING PEOPLE

General Electric didn't just "bring good things to life"; it brought good leaders to light. When former employees of the company got together for a reunion recently, they found that many of their old colleagues were now heads of large and small businesses across North America and the globe. They toasted GE and their great upbringing there.

A product of GE, even after he left his training ground, Larry Bossidy had a passion for talent. When he was CEO of Allied Signal and Honeywell, he ended each business review with a look at key talent. Standing across from Bossidy and his top team, the president of a subsidiary might summarize the numbers and do a quick analysis. But that was not enough. Methodically, Bossidy would ask questions about how good the talent was. Bam, bam, bam—he would go down the list of the business's top players. The underlying question to the person in charge was "How good are you at being critical and objective about your own people?" The meeting continued with probing questions, specific to the business yet broad enough to act as a barometer for how the leaders were developing.

On the basis of the answers, Bossidy would make long-term decisions about the top business leaders as well as his key talent and where they might move for development.

Success at all levels was measured by more than business trends and analysis: it depended on people and their development. A passion for talent became part of the corporate DNA at Allied Signal/Honeywell, just the way it had at GE. Nurturing talent can become part of your corporate culture as well:

- **Regularly include a discussion about people when business discussions occur.** Whenever you have a formal or informal meeting about organizational goals, try to include an ancillary discussion about the people who are implementing the objectives. How are they doing? How could they do better? What could get in their way? How should they deal with these things? What experiences would help them develop their skills and knowledge?

> *Nurturing talent can become part of your corporate culture.*

- **Ask probing questions of the leaders who report to you.** To determine how they are handling business issues, ask about what they've done with problems and standards. How is so-and-so dealing with quality control in outsourcing? Did the consultant he brought in fix the problems? To find out if they understand changing market conditions, ask what they know about the competition. To find out if they are being developed properly, ask what could make them fail. And don't forget to ask how they are developing the people who report to them!

Keeping your eyes on people as well as numbers is the best way to ensure the success of your organization. Very few organizations can run without people. Make sure that you find and develop the right ones to lead both now and in the future.

TRUTH 39

SUCCESSION PLANNING ENSURES
YOUR BENCH STRENGTH

Successful athletic teams make sure that they have good players "on the bench" waiting to go into the game when needed. Their coaches are continually thinking ahead about what might happen. How does the game or the season need to play out? What particular challenges is the team likely to face? What players will probably fade or stay on the injured list? The coaches select and prepare their backup players accordingly. To make the best decision, they work hard to know every member of their team individually, including their strengths and weaknesses.

Knowing your bench strength is a clear asset to any organization. As a business leader, you need to make sure that you have the right players on your bench to competently fill your team's jobs, now and in the future. Strategic planning allows you to successfully play out future strategy and challenges. For instance, if you are establishing operations in remote locations such as China, you may need players with cross-cultural skills and the ability to work independently.

Planning also helps you avoid a damaging leadership "vacuum" when someone leaves suddenly. Say your head of operations suddenly decides to leave for personal reasons. Could you immediately name possible replacement players? Maybe you have someone to keep things going, but is she good enough for the long haul?

Bringing in someone from the outside may resolve things, but historically, new people brought in near the top of the organization have a poor survival rate. It's hard for others to accept them. So avoid a mad scramble by thinking about the potential within your organization *now!*

Many organizations use a "succession planning" approach to manage leadership talent. This is done well in advance of any vacancies. Although methods vary, the core process involves assessing the strengths of your current workforce to identify a strong bench of candidates for possible future positions. On an organizational scale, a succession planning exercise cascades through every level of an organization. But nothing can stop you from doing it independently to manage the needs of your own department or team.

A succession planning discussion typically includes the following stages:

1. **Gathering your top team**—all the leaders and managers directly below you who have a sense of how your organization needs to work. Succession planning takes time, so schedule a half-day in a quiet room. It also requires focus and objectivity, so bringing in an outside facilitator helps ensure an effective process. Have participants think in advance about the strengths and weaknesses of the players who report to them.

2. **Establishing a discussion framework.** The main factors you want to assess people on are performance and potential. The precise meaning you attribute to these terms, particularly potential, is up to you. You may want to rank people on leadership potential, or you may have specific challenges or situations in mind that you want to judge their potential against, such as the Chinese expansion just mentioned. The important thing is to develop a shared understanding of those terms before initiating discussion.

   A nine-box grid helps keep the conversation on track, with one axis assigned to potential and another to performance. Each candidate is placed in one of the boxes. The structure forces participants to take a stand about where each player falls. However, the placement is not definitive or scientific. What really matters is the discussion and the qualitative conclusions you draw from it about where each player is going within the organization. Ranking them is just a tool to help you get there.

3. **Assessing the players.** Guided by the facilitator, participants should discuss each team member against the two criteria, placing that person on the grid. The success of the process depends heavily on people explaining their thinking. You need to carefully examine the precise nature of the candidate's performance and how he displays his potential. You look at both positive and negative, asking what goals he has successfully delivered, as well as the ways in which he might fail.

A heated discussion about where to place the players usually occurs. This is desirable, because the more you discuss each person, the more you evaluate his or her potential. The facilitator should ask for the evidence behind any assertions, ensuring that people are judged as objectively as possible. What you are ultimately hoping to identify are enough people who are high enough on each axis to fill future leadership needs. As the group discusses the players, you all talk about what positions they can fill now or in the future. Be sure that you discuss all the positions that report to you, as well as other important ones.

> *A heated discussion ... usually occurs. This is desirable, because the more you discuss each person, the more you evaluate his or her potential.*

What if a player you discuss is not quite ready for a more-responsible position? As part of the succession planning discussion, someone in the room must help identify the following:

- Specific jobs where the person can show that she can take on a challenging assignment by taking over a department or team that needs a turnaround

- Experiences such as a task force or a nonprofit board to broaden her skills and fill her gaps in strategic planning, for instance

- Training or other development opportunities to round out the person's skills, such as giving presentations

Your succession planning discussions are worth several hours of your and your team's time twice a year. This is a great way to keep developing your B players and ensure that your talent pipeline has players ready to move into the game whenever and wherever they're needed.

Succession planning is a great way to get you and your team thinking about the true state of your organizational leadership. But don't just make this a one-time exercise. The smartest leaders are continually thinking about bench strength. Jack Welch, former CEO of GE, was even known to keep assessments of his top executives in his top desk drawer so that he could review them regularly!

TRUTH 40

YOUR TEAM IS KEY TO YOUR SUCCESS, SO VET THEM WELL

We've all seen coaches drive their players during difficult games—running along the sidelines, waving their arms, or standing still and tense, chewing their knuckles. You can sense their desire to run on and fix the situation!

Organizational leaders share that frustration. As your teams go about their work, you see many things that could or should be done differently or faster. However, no matter how good you are, you can't do everything yourself. A great team is essential to the accomplishment of your goals, and it's your job to make that team great, freeing you up to lead.

Your core team consists of all the folks who report to you. When starting a leadership position, you put the best possible team in place by combining inherited members with strategic new hires. This team-building should be a slow, considered process. Your first act should be to carefully check or vet team members to determine whether you have the right people in the right jobs. Don't change anything until you have a sense of how the current members work on their own and together.

This initial period gives you the chance, as you develop your vision and goals, to think about the skills and knowledge required from your team. You also gain a sense of whether members either already have these or can acquire them. Whenever possible, it works best to nurture existing team members into new responsibilities rather than fire and hire.

Here are some ways to vet your team:

1. **Talking with others.** Informally interview as many people as possible—bosses, peers, associates, and clients—about your team's abilities to gain a variety of perspectives. Be aware that we see each other based on our own skills and needs, so don't take anyone's views at face value, and weigh the implications of their opinions. Tell your team what you're doing, explaining that you are getting a sense of everyone's strengths so that you can organize them in the best way.

> *Whenever possible, it works best to nurture existing team members into new responsibilities rather than fire and hire.*

2. **Observing your team.** Keep a careful eye out for how team members handle themselves under stress, work with others, and support the work you're doing. Don't jump to conclusions based on one incident; you never know what has affected them in a given situation, so build up a gradual picture.

3. **Testing your team.** Set team assignments that allow them to showcase their skills and abilities. For example,

have each team member show how well he or she can draw information from other departments to determine what the organization wants from a possible initiative or change. Then ask for their recommendations for what should happen next.

4. **Coaching your team.** Offer team members insights into their performance, and then note their capacity to change and grow in response. Remember, behaviors and motivation may change, but innate ability doesn't, so try to gain a sense of whether they are bright enough to learn from their own experiences, including mistakes and bad decisions.

After three months or so, you'll have a sense of how your team works, how individuals respond to your leadership, and how they learn from feedback. These criteria are key if you are to make decisions about who to keep and who to lose. Then, after about six months, it's time to make changes, letting go of team members who are no longer right for the job. This must be done sensitively, in close consultation with your legal and human resources experts.

You want excellent execution from your team. This requires great skills and experience, the ability to show grace under pressure, and a willingness to play ball. Last, but not least, they need to respect their coach: you!

TRUTH 41

DEDICATE YOUR COACHING TIME WHERE IT DOES THE MOST GOOD

"Leading would be great if it weren't for the people" is the kind of comment you hear all the time in organizations. It's true; people are complicated and unpredictable and take up a lot of time. Yet learning to accept their faults and work with their abilities is part of being a good leader. You wouldn't be a leader without them, so enjoy the challenge!

Coaching is one important way you can help your followers develop their skills. However, before embarking on a coaching program, you should keep two key things in mind. First, you can't coach everything. You can't make your staff perfect, so don't even try. Second, don't forget that the smallest of changes can make the biggest of differences.

The most rewarding coaching, for you and the individual, comes from focusing your energies in the areas where you can do the most good through the lightest touch, rather than trying to deal with the "big" issues. You'll most likely find that those bigger issues will start to resolve themselves as the smaller shifts come into effect. Just a small adjustment can make a good player excellent and help him or her get to the next level.

When starting a coaching program, identify areas where you can make a difference through your own observations, knowledge, and experience, and partly through listening to others' comments. If someone is known for his tendency to "wind people up," for instance, listen for his digs and then guide him in how to change. It's fairly easy to point out specific negative habits that may be holding back an employee. Process-oriented suggestions—guidance on how someone should do things—can also make a real impact. For instance, you might suggest using a checklist to make internal networking more methodical. Or encourage someone to schedule regular career development discussions with team members.

It's more difficult to tackle behaviors that come from ingrained habits or personality traits. For example, you may have a manager who slows down everyone's work by asking for in-depth details on

You can't make your staff perfect, so don't even try.

everything they do. It's likely that the manager feels the urge to do that at some basic level. Before addressing such traits, weigh the desirability of the change against the time and effort it would take to accomplish. If the person does not learn quickly, doesn't welcome coaching, or does not play a central role, it may be better to focus your efforts elsewhere.

In this case, if the slowdown is paralyzing a team, it might be worth it to intervene, but keep your aims modest. You can't alter the core character trait—that person will always need detail. But you *can* help someone understand how his behavior affects others and help him find practical ways in which he can manage that need in the workplace. For example, you might set up a framework in which a leader checks in with each team member only once a day. Likewise, don't try to introduce any changes that might come across as fake or phony. Smiling and acting warm and friendly are two particular areas that don't work when they're false.

The areas you can address most easily differ with each person. Some of the most rewarding and popular areas to work on include initiating and maintaining new networking relationships, reducing stress, and expressing oneself clearly and concisely. Try coaching an area, and see how your employee reacts. Is she interested, committed to change, or resistant?

Coaching is one of your most important jobs as a leader. Paying attention to what really matters helps your players get in shape to take on the challenges of organizational life. They will value your assistance in getting there.

TRUTH 42

AWKWARD DISCUSSIONS ARE TOUGH; PLAY OFFENSE, NOT DEFENSE

No matter how good you are at communicating, some discussions with your team members will be awkward. When you have to talk with them about issues that make them feel vulnerable—their reputations or their paychecks, for example—it can be difficult for them and for you.

Tackle these conversations by playing offense and not defense. That doesn't mean attacking others; it means taking charge of the situation. Initiate the conversation and direct it. Avoid having to take a defensive stance, in which the other person guides the conversation and you try to explain yourself or give examples. Focus on three areas: **what's realistic** given organizational constraints, **what's possible** going forward, and **what you want for yourself and others**.

Here are suggestions for dealing with three types of awkward conversations:

Performance reviews:

- **What's realistic** is to stick to discussion of general trends and observations. Reviews are not the time to argue about facts. Even fairly straightforward numeric facts are open to multiple interpretations. Don't get bogged down in a dispute over facts and specifics.

- **What's possible** is to work on two or three aspects of your subordinate's performance that will make a real difference, not every little thing you'd like to improve.

- **What you want** is to ensure that the overall review has been heard.

Bonus and pay discussions:

- **What's realistic** is what makes sense given the pool of money available for bonuses and salary increases. This is not the best time to bring up mistakes or other issues.

- **What's possible** is trying to keep these monetary rewards fair and consistent across your team and your organization. When you hear the objection that others have been better rewarded, you can say you'll investigate the issue and will keep it in mind for the next time. There is no perfect reward structure.

- **What you want** is for the other person to realize that you're trying to keep things fair and consistent while rewarding them appropriately.

Don't get bogged down in a dispute over facts and specifics.

Correcting errors and mistakes:

- **What's realistic** is for you to discuss these in performance reviews and coaching conversations as part of a broader pattern of behaviors.

- **What's possible** is to agree on steps to make sure the errors or mistakes don't happen again.
- **What you want** is for your discussion to empower your team member to use new ways of working so that he or she doesn't make the same mistake twice.

In these conversations, no one is right, and no one is wrong; no one wins or loses. You want your subordinate and your organization to move forward successfully and smoothly. Keep reminding yourself of this if you are tempted to defend your position or your thinking.

PART IX

THE TRUTH ABOUT YOUR LEADERSHIP REPUTATION

TRUTH 43

IDEAS COME ACROSS DIFFERENTLY
WITH DIFFERENT MEDIA

The classic image of the newshound stalking a scoop through the city streets is an anachronism. Today's reporters cruise the Internet for news via blogs and podcasts, keeping up with new communication technology. Take a page from their book.

Whatever your organization, communication media matter. They are the means through which messages about your organization, good and bad, are transmitted to the outside world. Even if you don't actively seek out media or press opportunities, they will find you.

Once your company has a profile in the outside world, others—including journalists—take an interest in what you're doing. That interest isn't just in the positive. The press, for example, doesn't just report what you want it to, but selects what it thinks will interest readers and viewers. It's your job to package and position your company information so that it's picked up when and how you want.

Dealing with media effectively requires a good understanding of the different forms and their practices. Each information delivery method requires a different approach to getting your message out. To use media effectively, keep the following points in mind.

Print Media

Newspapers and magazines carry general overviews of news in brief alongside in-depth features on particularly interesting areas. Find out which publications are most relevant to your organization by researching their readership and reading their editorials. Then capture their attention by thinking up angles to pique readers' interest, summing these up in a press release to be faxed or e-mailed to the publication. Don't just wait for big news items; keep the press informed of changes such as new staff appointments. This is a good source of publicity for your organization. In fact, giving media sources interesting tidbits from time to time creates a relationship with them for future connections.

Even if you don't actively seek out media or press opportunities, they will find you.

Visual Media

Visual images grab people's attention and linger in their memories. Studies have shown that people remember much more of what they see than what they hear. You should therefore carefully invest resources in generating the best possible images—still and moving—of you and your organization, ensuring that these are symbolic of what you want people to remember.

Moving images (video footage) are more prevalent, shown not only on television but via the Internet, and even downloaded to phones and iPods. It is therefore more important than ever to have professionally prepared, up-to-date video footage on hand. It's worth paying for some training so that you feel confident before the camera and can articulate your message clearly and concisely.

New Media

The Internet or World Wide Web has become one of the principal ways of sharing information, news, and opinions. The Web portal Google is used so often as a real-time, evolving encyclopedia that "to google" is now a verb. The first thing many people do when researching a company or individual is to type the name into an Internet search engine and see what comes up.

Having a well-designed and up-to-date Web site is essential for any contemporary organization. Many companies use their Web front page as their news page to convey events to others quickly and easily, without their having to trawl through the whole site. The trick is to keep each piece of news brief (people don't like to read long pieces of text on-screen) and to offer links to as many points of interest as possible. And keep your news up to date. There's nothing worse than old news hanging around when your organization has up-to-the-minute news that needs to be reported.

The other Internet feature to consider is the blog. Blogs, or Web logs, are online journals maintained on a dizzying range of topics by anyone who can master the basic technology. This means that you need to pay attention not only to what you place on the Internet, but also what others say about you. Blogs wield increasing influence with consumers; it takes only one popular blogger expressing an online grievance with your company to cause a whole host of public relations problems. Get your computer technician to set up a Really Simple Syndication (RSS) feed to allow you to keep track of what's new on the Web in your areas of interest, including your company. That way, you'll avoid nasty surprises.

Understanding the particular characteristics of each communication avenue helps you get your message across effectively. It pays to anticipate the needs of reporters and researchers and to package news in ways that make it easy to understand and communicate.

TRUTH 44

YOU CAN'T HIDE THE SUN WITH YOUR HAND: BE HONEST

Have you ever read something important about your organization in the newspaper before it was announced internally? Or heard a bit of gossip from the grapevine that you should have learned from your boss? If you have, you know how frustrating it is. You feel excluded from the organization's core information flow and, by extension, not valued by your bosses. Worse, it can damage your trust in your organization, making you wary of committing to its work.

When you become a leader, you see this issue from two sides. It's important to keep some information confidential. However, it's also important to let people know what's happening—not just employees, but also external observers such as press. A basic rule of thumb in this information age is to keep nothing but the most sensitive information secret. Hiding information can negatively affect a company's reputation. Once information leaks out—and leak out it will— it can quickly spread around the globe via the Internet, or even by old-fashioned word of mouth, in ways over which you have no control. It's therefore in your best interest to get as much information out there as you can, in a way that suits you, as soon as it's possible to share it.

When it comes to internal communication, follow these principles:

- Details of individuals' personal lives, their salaries, or job situations should *always* be kept confidential.

- Good news, such as business wins and employee appointments, should always be shared quickly.

- It's also vital to let people know quickly about losses and bad news, before they hear it from someone else.

It's quite likely that the second and third cases (particularly the third) will generate external interest as well, from the press and the public. In those cases, you need to ensure that you share the news internally first. With good news, you usually have some control over when the story breaks. Use the time to shape what you want to say, and vet it with others. Then share it first with those it directly affects before announcing it more widely via e-mail, briefing, or your preferred internal communication method, and then externally via a news release.

Bad news is more challenging. You usually don't have the luxury of time, because bad news leaks out quickly, so don't wait to have everything lined up before you share news internally. It's just better that people hear the facts directly from you, especially if their livelihoods are at stake. Give them those facts in as calm and positive a way as possible. That doesn't mean putting a gloss on things or being deceitful, but presenting the facts in a straight and unemotional way and being ready, where possible, with ideas on how to bounce back. Your comments need to be honest and human. "Human" is admitting when you make mistakes and telling the truth, even when it hurts.

Even with bad news, don't wait for the press to come to you. Once you have dealt with internal communications, be proactive and go to the press! Preempting their interest allows you to shape the discussion. Address the outside world in "real" words, not words sanitized by your legal team. If your organization goofed, admit it. Deal with any criticism in a nondefensive way. If you don't have the answers yet, say so. If you need to talk about something that may have legal implications, check with lawyers, but quickly. Taking too much time makes you look as if you're hiding something. Whatever you do, don't say "No comment." That's a red flag for listeners.

If your organization goofed, admit it. Deal with any criticism in a nondefensive way.

Being honest pays off. Every U.S. president who has admitted mistakes to the American people has seen his approval rating go up. This has worked for Ronald Reagan, Bill Clinton, and especially John F. Kennedy, who saw his rating almost double to 84% after he discussed the Bay of Pigs incident.

A great corporate example of honesty with the press and the public, which set the standard for bad news management, was Johnson & Johnson's handling of the Tylenol poisonings. In 1982, when some of its capsules were contaminated, the company immediately issued public warnings and pulled every bottle of the medicine from store shelves, restoring confidence in the organization. The company quickly regained, and even increased, its market share.

Above all, when it comes to both employees and external media, the golden rule is *never lie*. If you're caught in a lie, you'll never be trusted again.

TRUTH 45

SPOUSES AND PARTNERS MUST BE ON THEIR BEST BEHAVIOR

In 1946 the British Foreign Office published a manual for leaders' wives. Instructions were specific. Couples were to arrive exactly five minutes before official events. Husbands and wives were never to stand together at these events, but to mingle. The wife of a lower-ranking official should never introduce herself to a wife of a higher-ranking official without permission. The "top" wife would even complete report cards on the conduct of her fellow wives!

Although times have changed, some traditions remain. Whether you're the CEO or the head of a department, at home or abroad, your partner needs to be a model of appropriate behavior. Just as the employees you pick for your team reflect your leadership judgment and ability, so does your spouse or partner. Everything he or she says and does in public is a reflection of you. It's therefore worth ensuring that your partner is aware of the "rules."

In this contemporary age, the topic of spouse or partner behavior may appear a delicate or controversial one. It's important to realize that, by and large, the issue is no longer one of subordination of women (although women are still often expected to supervise the entertaining!). Rules now apply to men too. And the nature of the expected behavior has evolved. Today's observers are not so much looking for obedience as they are for a companion who is obviously worthy of the leader.

At company events, that means being witty and entertaining and never short of something interesting to say, rather than just smiling nicely and chatting about the weather. It also still requires the spouse or partner to be well mannered and well dressed and to comport himself or herself with dignity no matter what his or her personal style. Tact and discretion are vital too.

Jim, head of a U.S. pharmaceutical company for Asia and Australia, invited his boss, visiting from Philadelphia, to dinner at their home. The food was delicious, and the conversation flowed, but, over dessert, Jim's wife Louise started to complain about the late-night calls her husband had to make to the States. She also raised the issue of Jim's never-ending travel schedule visiting the countries in his region. Didn't the company understand how much time this took up? Her young children barely knew their father.

Everything he or she says and does in public is a reflection of you.

Jim's boss was horrified. For him, these tasks were just part of the expatriate package, giving Jim broad experience and the chance to prove his skills and commitment to the company. He began to wonder if Jim was up to the job, and he decided not to mention the possible promotion he had been considering. The meal went on, and ostensibly all was fine, but a fault line had been opened in Jim's relationship with his employers.

Those early etiquette books for spouses were full of do's and don'ts. Here are some for contemporary times, with a focus on corporate entertaining. If your partner is committed to your career, why not tactfully share them with him or her? It's your job to make life easier for your loved one and to help with the details, particularly if you are new to your position. But don't forget that whatever is important for a spouse also applies to you!

Here are some **do's** for today's corporate spouses and partners:

- Behave graciously with staff at all levels by paying them personal attention and always being polite. Staff members tend to talk with other staff! Use small courtesies to shape a positive reputation.

- Plan your conversation before social events. Read the day's paper, for instance, or rerun in your head interesting events of the past couple of weeks and how you might relate them to others.

Here are some **don'ts** for today's corporate spouses and partners:

- Don't divulge your opinions about your spouse's job unless you've discussed and rehearsed what you'll say. People will remember what you say.

- Don't complain about anyone or anything work related at a social event. Stay neutral to positive. If you want to express frustration, do so privately at home, where your comments won't affect your partner's reputation.

- Don't disagree with anyone from your partner's work (or your partner) in public. Resentment may linger.

Although they're not on the payroll, spouses and partners play an important role in your leadership reputation. The two of you can be a united team inside and outside the office. The question of whether unmarried or same-sex couples need to abide by the same set of rules depends on the organization's norms and values and your location in the world. Your personal setup is part of your leadership role. Plan and prepare for what makes sense for you and your organization.

TRUTH 46

YOU DON'T GET YOUR MEAT WHERE YOU GET YOUR POTATOES

In 2005, Boeing CEO Harry Stonecipher resigned following revelations of a liaison with a female employee. An investigation by internal and external legal counsel had determined his actions to be inconsistent with the Boeing Code of Conduct. Stonecipher's board was forced to conclude that his actions showed poor judgment, calling into question his ability to lead. After 32 years of company service, Stonecipher was asked to leave.

"You don't get your meat where you get your potatoes" is an old maxim about office relationships. It's a crass way of saying that you should avoid intimate encounters on the job. This advice is particularly important for top-level leaders, who must set the standards for others to follow. The Boeing Code, for example, demands unimpeachable professional and personal behavior from a CEO. It's no accident that this sounds like the guidelines for a U.S. president. The higher you go as a leader, the tougher the rules.

You might be thinking, "I'm single, and I'm too busy for a social life. Why shouldn't I enjoy the company of a like-minded person I meet at work?" Stop right there! It's true that there

The higher you go as a leader, the tougher the rules.

have always been workplace romances, and most likely there always will be. A large percentage of people meet their future spouses at work. But once you reach a certain level in the hierarchy, it's in your best interests to resist the temptation. There is little room for error. Should you find it impossible to resist, at least have the self-control to ensure that one of you resigns or moves to another organization before the news goes public.

As a leader, you are seen as having considerable power and influence over others. Showing a special interest in anyone can lead to accusations of favoritism at best, especially if any promotion or pay raise might be linked to it, and sexual harassment at worst. It hardly needs to be said that these are huge no-nos for a leader. In the past, concern about this led many capable women to be barred from jobs requiring close working relationships with older, more powerful men. They also were barred from participating in off-site conferences. These circumstances may have relaxed, but the principle hasn't.

You are also too visible to be able to conduct an intimate relationship with others. Colleagues and employees will spot things that would pass unnoticed in others, making it impossible to keep a liaison secret. Stonecipher's indiscretion was swiftly noticed and was revealed to the board via an anonymous letter. Such visibility means that not only should you not conduct a relationship, but you should beware of showing any hint of affection or intimacy. Friendly or warm behavior can easily be misconstrued, leading to trouble. Be compassionate and kind, but not overly friendly. This is particularly important with employees from some other cultures, such as China, where public touching between genders is viewed as indiscreet.

To protect your reputation and that of your organization, you need to be committed to strong ethical leadership. Whether or not what you're doing is improper, your appearance must be above suspicion.

TRUTH 47

When the newly minted managing director was told that there was unfavorable "corridor talk" about him and his organization, he asked, "Which corridor?" He was wise enough to know that it didn't matter if there was a bit of "noise" about him; what mattered was who was listening to what. People often think that where there's smoke, there's fire, but that's not always true of office gossip.

Whenever human beings are grouped, they talk—and often complain—about each other. At work, such chatter is usually simple background noise, but at times it can tip off leaders to critical problems in the organization.

Learning to distinguish important talk from inconsequential noise is not easy, but it is well worth the effort. When confronted with a troubling piece of information, leaders should do the following:

- **Consider the speaker's motivation.** Is he or she just trying to be the center of attention, perhaps at the expense of a rival? Or is the speaker reasonably impartial?

- **Be careful not to take information as the truth about someone,** even when it comes from a trusted place, like your human resources department. Remember that a particularly juicy piece of gossip may spread throughout your organization very quickly, so information that seems to be corroborated by many people could all come from the same faulty source.

- **Model the behavior you want to see in your organization.** You don't want others to overreact or jump to conclusions, so don't let your followers see you doing so. Keep your comments about people objective, neutral, and related to work. Pay attention to noise as an early warning, but don't get flustered or obsessed by it.

Often the most valuable message in office chatter is not about the person being discussed. For instance, suppose someone who has done a great job for you is now talked about as sucking up or having a leg up. Maybe you said something positive about him in public or thanked him

> *Pay attention to noise as an early warning, but don't get flustered or obsessed by it.*

without thanking others. The real message in this chatter is for you: Don't make so much of a fuss over one person's contribution that others feel let down.

Sometimes, though, office gossip or its written equivalent—the anonymous letter—can let you know that someone's work behavior is unacceptable. If someone is taking bribes, for instance, or having an affair that affects his or her coworkers, there is a compelling need for you to investigate, even though the complaint was not made through official channels. One company saved itself from serious consequences when it acted on an anonymous tip that a company attorney was harassing female employees in China. The investigation forestalled a threatened class-action lawsuit at the company's U.S. headquarters.

There are times to pay attention to office "noise" immediately and times to watch and wait, times to question and times to squelch gossip. Wise leaders learn to tell the difference.

PART X

THE TRUTH ABOUT YOUR CONNECTIONS

TRUTH 48

YOU CAN'T MICROWAVE YOUR LEADERSHIP RELATIONSHIPS

T he gadgets in our lives have made us accustomed to instant results. Thanks to your microwave oven, you can have a hot meal any time, day or night, in a matter of seconds. But some things still cannot be rushed. If you want a soufflé, there's no way around it: you have to take it slow.

Leadership relationships are like that. When moving into a new leadership role, you have to let meaningful connections develop gradually. Wise leaders don't just jump in and start telling people what to do. They devote the first 90 days of their tenure to establishing new—and refreshing old —relationships with all key players. This builds confidence and trust so that those relationships are primed and ready and don't fall flat just when you need them. It also means that you don't tread on anyone's toes.

Take Geoffrey, who became head of a Midwestern oil services company following a two-year stint as president of Indonesian operations. Geoffrey had been with the company for 18 years, but he knew that after having been away it was vital to rebuild old relationships and create new ones.

Try drawing a map of all current and potential relationships within your organization.

During his first months, Geoffrey got to know his team. He asked for their thoughts about what was working and what wasn't. He listened, and he acted when he could make a difference. He made small changes such as removing obstructionist bosses and creating office space, and he consulted with his growing network about larger changes for the future. He also established connections with people outside his organization, making overtures to political figures in Washington, and volunteering to chair an American Petroleum Institute committee. Knowing that the VP was concerned about Mexico's oil industry, Geoffrey also went to Mexico City and brought back up-to-date information from his contacts there.

In all of this, Geoffrey didn't forget to make midnight phone calls to his colleagues in Indonesia to update them. By the end of those 90 days, he had laid a solid groundwork of new and continuing relationships that boded well for the future. His success offers lessons for anyone moving into a leadership role:

1. **Identify connections that will be vital to you in your new role.**

   Internally: Try drawing a map of all current and potential relationships within your organization. Put yourself at the center, with the others in a circle around you. They may include your boss and his or her colleagues, your colleagues, groups that support you (such as communications and human resources), and your direct reports.

Externally: Do the same for your external relationships. Depending on your job, you may want to create or reinforce relationships with your professional society, politicians, consultants, vendors, and academics or experts.

Background research—talking to people you know or looking on the Internet—is useful in establishing who's who. Knowing something about someone before you meet him or her also shows that you care about the relationship and gives you a point of contact.

2. **Consult with people and share your plans.** Once you've identified and researched those vital connections, approach people for information and input. Many will have valuable insights that will help craft your leadership vision and agenda. As you establish the key elements of your strategy, continue to check in with those people, internal and external, who are most involved in or affected by your strategy, running your plans by them at the end of the 90 days. This lets people know that you've been listening and shows them how you plan to move forward with their input.

3. **Keep it up.** After your initial information-gathering period, it may be tempting to let some relationships slide, but maintaining them is a wise investment, because you never know when you may need them. Consider having your assistant monitor a list of your key contacts so that you can schedule regular, brief conversations with them.

Taking the time to build and renew relationships early on in your tenure is essential. It is through your relationships that you get things done. Be sure to make them a top priority.

TRUTH 49

YOUR NETWORK IS YOUR LIFELINE TO INFLUENCE AND INFORMATION

I magine that you get a phone call at six o'clock on a Saturday night from your technical staff, saying there has been a sudden rise in pollution in a river near one of your manufacturing plants. Even though you're pretty sure your organization didn't do the polluting, it looks bad, and it's bad for the environment. You believe that the local water-processing facilities need a heads-up about the pollution type and location so that they can deal with it fast. But they don't know you from Adam. How do you get a speedy cleanup?

If you've spent time getting to know all the important experts and politicians who can help your organization, you're ahead of the game. You're even better off if you've covered all your bases by doing small favors and by keeping important players informed about anything that could affect pollution in the locations where you do business.

If the press gets hold of the pollution information, they could have a field day with speculation. As it happens, they don't get that information because you call the governor, who calls for federal help to combat the pollution quickly. The municipal water supply is saved by a quick intervention by experts you met at a conference on water safety.

The more influential your leadership position, the more you need to establish relationships with people in the know and people who have clout. A large, informal network yields dividends in many ways. Your network is a diverse group of people in the know—contacts gathered over time who are there when you need them. You can rely on them to give you straight information, whether you need to connect with your state's governor on a weekend, find a new employee, learn how to do business in a new location, or get attention from a national newspaper. You establish these connections all the time by seeking out others as thinking partners—people with whom you can talk things over and who can give you feedback and opinions. It's important to know people who have connections both inside and outside your organization.

Once you find good people, professionals or not, nurture these relationships by using them regularly, honoring their guidance, and keeping them informed. You may want to use them when you aren't desperate for help so that they take your call when you are. You need to vet your network all the time to confirm that these people are still right for you. Ask yourself whether the people in your network respond to you in a timely manner and make an effort to keep you in the know. Last but not least, are they committed to keeping

A large, informal network yields dividends in many ways.

confidential information confidential and loyal enough not to talk about you behind your back? It's tempting to spill juicy information about well-known organizations and leaders. Watch for loose lips!

TRUTH 50

PEERS AND POWER ARE A POTENT MIX

Have you ever walked into a locker room or a martial arts class? The smell that hits you is that of competition and sweat. In meeting rooms in organizations around the world, the dynamics, if not the aroma, are similar, as peers jockey for power in an adult version of sports competition.

When you enter a leadership role, it's important to realize that the organizational game has changed. Your new peers may now see you as competition. It's no accident that on feedback questionnaires of all kinds, peers tend to mark each other below scores received from bosses and direct reports.

It's usually not personal. A certain amount of distrust is natural, because, now or in the future, you and your peers will be in direct competition for roles, resources, and remuneration. And it's OK—indeed, healthy—to develop some caution regarding the motivation and moves of your peers. Otherwise, you could be in for a nasty surprise.

Consider Albert, who relied on another department's research and fact-finding capabilities. He soon found that their reports could be biased and that they did not give his group enough information.

Frustrated, he openly complained about the research department and refused to continue using its reports. But Albert soon realized he was burning bridges with his actions. He backed off and approached the problem differently.

Using feedback gleaned from asking his clients what they thought, he let the research department know how the biases and omissions in its previous reports had upset his clients. When the emphasis was on serving clients, not on helping a peer and possible competitor, the research department recognized and responded to the need to cooperate.

Given that resources are usually stretched and the interests of departments often don't coincide, developing trust with peers is tricky. Ideally,

A certain amount of distrust is natural.

trust comes from knowing that a peer can put the organization's interests before his or her own and will give credit to other departments rather than taking total ownership.

But don't take it for granted that a peer will always act this way. Establish clear guidelines and expectations for your work together. For instance, if you have to split a commission, agree on the percentage split in advance. And constantly monitor your joint efforts, giving quick feedback about what's working and what isn't if your peers' work diverges from the framework you set up.

In Albert's case, he found that providing clear guidelines and expectations backed by others was the first step in creating a good peer group relationship. He also learned that he had to communicate constantly with and test the research team to be sure they were working toward compatible goals.

Remember, a peer today may be a boss tomorrow. So keep it clean and clear. You'll be glad you did.

TRUTH 51

IT'S LONELY AT THE TOP;
KEEP IT THAT WAY

People may have said to you that the higher you go in an organization, the lonelier it gets. Does it have to be this way? The answer is yes.

When you reach the top, you cannot afford to be too open with anyone inside or close to your organization. You can no longer treat any conversation as casual or confidential. And you certainly cannot talk through challenges you are facing with colleagues in the same way as before. Once you're a leader, everything you say, however inconsequential, has more weight to others' ears and, as it tends to get repeated, more potential reverberations. It's therefore important that you find a few trusted people—"thinking partners"—with whom you can share concerns and half-formed thoughts, without fear that these may be used against you.

This is partly about confidentiality. Some information is clearly meant to be kept quiet. Other information is not officially private but may have unforeseen consequences if shared. The most innocent of remarks may play out badly when repeated to a boss or board member. It's therefore best to apply a need-to-know policy when talking with others. Be alert not

> *A casual comment can easily stray onto the organizational grapevine.*

only for accidental breaches of confidence, but also for others looking for ways to weaken your position. Former colleagues who wanted your job may well have knives out for you until you securely establish your leadership.

Being lonely at the top also means not discussing ideas or strategies with others until you have thought them through. Sharing ideas in their formative stages can result in their being misconstrued or misquoted. Many people also associate unformed ideas with uninformed thinking and lack of confidence. These are the last things you want others to think about you as a leader. Likewise, you need to take care with whom you share concerns, especially when these are about other colleagues and employees. A casual comment can easily stray onto the organizational grapevine, leaving you looking unprofessional, or damaging relationships if word gets too far.

So with whom can you talk things through? Ideally, your thinking partners are people with at least as much experience and knowledge as you. The more accomplished they are, the better they can assist you in making the right decisions. Those who also perform, or have performed, your role are superb. Coaches or consultants can also be good bets. Both types of partner can be found through professional networks. However, whomever you choose, remember that some things should always be confidential—unless protected by safeguards such as the attorney-client relationship—and that finding a good thinking partner is not a license to share absolutely anything.

One final word: Spouses and partners do not make good thinking partners.

Supportive as they may be, they do not always understand organizational dynamics or the need for confidentiality. Consider the wife who refused to shake her husband's boss's hand because of some former slight—long-forgotten by the employee, but not by the wife—thus doing career damage by making it clear that some behind-the-scenes complaining had been going on. This doesn't mean that you can't let loved ones know how you're feeling, but be careful what you share.

Having to guard your tongue is part of the price of leadership. Everyone needs to talk about what they're going through, but wise leaders learn to pick their confidants carefully and, when in doubt, keep quiet.

TRUTH 52

TRUST AND LOYALTY ARE LONG-TERM GOALS

Y ou need people you can trust. But how do you get them? Although it might seem ideal to surround yourself with people you have known for years, that may not be the best option for new leaders. Even if it is, it may not be wise to cordon yourself off from new ideas. It pays to put in the time and effort to build mutual trust with your team and colleagues in your leadership position. This reciprocity is essential in the workplace; however efficient you are, you can't do your job in isolation.

There is no formula for generating trust. Trust is a gut feeling, something that evolves through shared experiences. However, in building effective trust at work, it can be helpful to consider what kind of trust you need in whom.

There are four major types of trust to think about as you work with others:

- **Get-it-done trust** involves knowing that others, such as your team, will meet commitments on time and within budget and will alert you to any potential delay. This is vital with anyone else to whom you delegate tasks. You test this kind of trust by making small requests and noting how and when people get them done. Then you'll know who you can trust when a crucial project with an inflexible deadline comes along. You can nurture a climate of get-it-done trust by making it clear that people should come to you with any concerns about meeting deadlines as soon as they have them.

- **Expertise trust** occurs when you can depend on someone's special knowledge or ability. It is vital with any experts with whom you work. You must be certain that their advice is sound and their knowledge current. For example, when hiring a consultant to advise you, you should check that his or her experience includes the kinds of situations your organization may face. You need to know that experts will give you the real scoop and the whole scoop whenever you ask or even before you do. You test expertise trust by double-checking the information you are given until you feel confident in someone. That's especially important when you're in other countries, where your gut feelings may not be as accurate.

- **Political savvy trust** comes from knowing that your team and colleagues understand workplace norms and how to play the organizational game. It is bound up with confidentiality and discretion and is important in any colleague with whom you work in confidential ways. Being great at getting things done, or being experts in their field, is no guarantee that colleagues deserve political savvy trust. Your creative staff member who comes up with great off-the-wall ideas may not realize the importance of keeping these ideas low-profile so that her staff doesn't think they're a done deal until they have been vetted and passed by others.

■ **Structural trust** is needed whenever you work with people from elsewhere in your company. It comes from knowing that someone in another department can put the entire organization's interests before his or her own and give credit to other departments rather than taking total ownership. Since resources are often stretched, and different departmental interests often don't coincide, developing total structural trust is tricky. You can generate a good working trust by establishing clear frameworks in advance rather than taking leaps of faith. You should agree on how to resolve conflicts between departments before the need arises. If you have a policy or procedures in place that help you help your team members "play fair" when they work across the white spaces on the organization chart, it is easier for everyone to develop trust.

Think of the ways new colleagues can earn your trust, and then open those paths for them.

Each occasion for dealing with others, however low-key, is a chance to test their trustworthiness. Give new people a chance to prove themselves. If someone breaks your trust once, you should be wary of asking for his or her support with anything important in the future. But try not to get hung up on a single incident: you're looking at behavior over time. When someone tells you something you don't want to hear, that's not a break in trust. It shows how trustworthy that person is, because it's in your best interests to get a heads-up about other ways of thinking.

Think of the ways new colleagues can earn your trust, and then open those paths for them. Trust develops over time. Be conscious of earning and granting trust as you work with people in your organization. Others will repay you.

REFERENCES

FURTHER READING

Part I: The Truth About Assuming a Leadership Position

1. **More Responsible Roles Require More Mental "Bandwidth"**

   Elliot Jaques, an influential thinker about organizations, leadership, and management (and formulator of the term *mid-life crisis*!), writes excellently on strategic thinking. Jaques makes it clear that the real key to success is not the number of people or pennies, but your cognitive capability. Jaques, Elliot and Clement, Stephen D., ***Executive Leadership: A Practical Guide to Managing Complexity***, Cason Hall & Co Pub, 1991, is one of his more accessible works and had a powerful impact upon U.S. Army leadership. More theoretical, but worth the effort, is his classic work Jaques, Elliot, ***Requisite Organization: A Total System for Effective Managerial Organization and Managerial Leadership for the 21st Century***: ***Amended,*** Cason Hall & Co Pub, 1998. This is a book you have to read and reread. For another take on the mental juggling that you are required to do as a leader, try Weick, Karl E, and Sutcliffe, Kathleen M.,

Managing the Unexpected: Assuring High Performance in an Age of Complexity, Jossey-Bass, 2001, with its focus on mindfulness, encouraging leaders to stay alert to, and focused on, subtle warnings of change or crisis ahead. I can also recommend Fairtlough, Gerard, "Innovation and Organization" in Dodgson, Mark and Rothwell, Roy (eds.), *The Handbook of Industrial Innovation*, Edward Elgar Publishing Company, 1994, for good strategic thinking about how you structure your organization as a leader.

2. **Inheriting an Assistant Requires Re-Education**

   Bolton, Robert and Grover Bolton, Dorothy, *People Styles at Work: Making Bad Relationships Good and Good Relationships Better*, American Management Association, 1996, is an oldie but a goodie on this subject. Over many years and editions, I've found that managers love this book for its advice on working out how others prefer to communicate. Hay, Julie, *Working It Out at Work: Understanding Attitudes and Building Relationships*, Sherwood Publishing, 1994, is a good general book on productive working relationships, with lots of practical suggestions.

3. **Staffing Your Leadership Office: Your Assistant Plays a Vital Role**

   Leaders often really struggle with this issue, but it is vital that you carefully vet, or test, anyone you are hiring. This chapter is based on the bad experiences leaders have had and the "Smart" interview format articulated by Brad Smart in Smart, Bradford D., *Topgrading: How Leading*

Companies Win by Hiring, Coaching and Keeping the Best People, Prentice Hall Press, 1999. The interview technique is the best around for defining what you want and ensuring you get it. It's worth the price of the book and will help you ensure that all your hires are "A players."

4. **The Gaps in Your Personal Work Habits Show Up When You Move Up**

There are a number of excellent books on the market that will hold your hand and offer you wise and well-researched advice through those difficult early days as a fledgling leader. My favorites are Gabarro, John G., *The Dynamics of Taking Charge,* Harvard Business School Press, 1987, which pinpoints the reasons for new managers succeeding or failing; Ciampa, Dan and Watkins, Michael, *Right From The Start: Taking Charge in a New Leadership Role*, Harvard Business School Press, 1999, with its focus on the particular challenges faced by a leader joining a new company; Hill, Linda, A., *Becoming a Manager: How New Managers Master the Challenges of Leadership (Second Edition)*, Harvard Business School Press, 2003; and Bennis, Warren, *On Becoming a Leader: The Leadership Classic—Updated and Expanded*, Perseus Publishing, 2003, which stresses the importance of self-reflection and knowing yourself if you are to be a good leader.

5. **A Resource-Based View of Your Organization Goes Beyond the Numbers**

Kim Warren of The London Business School is really the only person to look at for this. The concept of strategy dynamics can be tough to come to grips with, but it's worth persevering. I can honestly say that taking a course with him changed my view of how business interacts and how I could influence it. Warren, Kim, *Competitive Strategy Dynamics*, John Wiley and Sons, 2002, shows how to use a "resource map" to understand and then plan your business.

Part II: The Truth About Effective Leadership Styles

6. Soft-Spoken Leadership Requires Stamina

An influential book referred to in this chapter is Collins, Jim, *Good to Great: Why Some Companies Make the Leap... and Others Don't*, Collins, 2001. One of the reasoned findings of this roadmap to success is that the most effective leaders are often humble and strong-willed rather than outgoing. In addition, Badaracco Jr., Joseph, L., *Leading Quietly*, Harvard Business School Press, 2002, tells you how to do exactly that, offering examples of great quiet leaders from history, and stressing how restraint and modesty, when coupled with tenacity, can deliver on behalf of your business. One of those great quiet leaders, mentioned in the chapter, was Abraham Lincoln. If you'd like to find out more about his style, I suggest Phillips, Donald T., *Lincoln on Leadership: Executive Strategies for Tough Times*, Warner Books, 1993, for some solid advice. Finally, if you want a quick, yet informed read on the subject of quiet leadership, seek out the following article: Mintzberg, Henry, "Managing Quietly" in *Leader to Leader*, 12, Spring 1999, pp.24-30.

7. **Bullshit Makes Good Fertilizer—Just Watch Your Step**

The writer and thinker who has done most to put bullshit into the public realm is Harry G. Frankfurt, with his humorous yet philosophical take on the prevalence of hot air (or worse) in contemporary life: Frankfurt, Harry G., *On Bullshit*, Princeton University Press, 2005. Frankfurt focuses on the negatives of this trait. Other books that may prove more helpful practically are those advising the reader on how to generate working conditions in which creativity and imagination can flourish. A classic in this field is de Bono, Edward, *Six Thinking Hats*, Back Bay Books, 1999, offering techniques for groups to stimulate new ideas and ways of looking at things. He advocates an open and playful discussion style. Others who have proved their mettle in an organizational context, and that may help you become a better bullshitter, are Michalko, Michael, *Cracking Creativity: The Secrets of Creative Genius*, Ten Speed Press, 2001, and von Oech, *A Whack on the Side of The Head: How You Can Be More Creative*, Warner Business Books, 1998.

8. **Player/Coach Is a Tricky Role: Make Sure That You Do Both Well**

There are some very good books out there looking at how to develop excellent teams and team-working, directed at both those who run teams from the outside and those keen to direct things from the middle. Player-coaches may find O'Brien, Maureen, *Who's Got the Ball (and Other Nagging Questions About Team Life): A Player's*

Guide for Work Teams, Jossey-Bass, 1995, a useful prompt. This down-to-earth guide to playing as a team and being a good team member may help you find the balance between directing and doing. For those days when you have your coach's hat on, Doyle, James S., *The Business Coach: A Game Plan for the New Work Environment*, Wiley, 1999, helps managers more used to a top-down approach come to grips with today's more collaborative leadership styles. I've also heard good things about Augur, Philip and Palmer, Joy, *Player Manager: Rise of Professionals Who Manage While They Work*, Texere, 2003, which offers detailed case studies on professionals operating in that situation.

9. **Caring Leaders Treat Their Teams Like Family**

The concept of the caring leader is well articulated in Kouzes, James M., and Posner, Barry Z., *Encouraging the Heart: A Leader's Guide to Rewarding and Recognizing Others*, Jossey-Bass, 2003. This stresses that caring is not about grand gestures and big smiles, but about clear systems of rewards and appreciation. Caring becomes particularly important when times are tough or change is occurring in an organization, and the leader may need to take particular actions in those circumstances. Two texts that offer good advice from this perspective are Lombardo, Michael M. and Eichinger Robert W., *Preventing Derailment: What to Do Before It's Too Late*, CCL Press, 1989, and Lee Marks, Mitchell, *Charging Back Up the Hill: Workplace Recovery After Mergers, Acquisitions and Downsizing*, Jossey-Bass,

2003. Both suggest ways to get jaded employees back on track.

10. **Innovation Requires Preparation**

    The skilled innovator manages to locate the perfect middle ground between high creativity and rigorous planfulness. This is not easy! Thinking that may help you with this task is provided by Christensen, Clayton M., Overdorf, Michael, Macmillan, Ian, and McGrath, Rita, *Harvard Business Review on Innovation*, Harvard Business School Press, 2001, a good overall primer; Dundon, Elaine, *The Seeds of Innovation: Cultivating the Synergy That Fosters New Ideas*, American Management Association, 2002, which stresses a message of discipline and strategy; and Davila, Tony, Epstein, Mark J., and Shelton, Robert, *Making Innovation Work: How to Manage It, Measure It, and Profit from It*, Wharton School Publishing, 2005, which places emphasis on, and provides examples of, the processes that lead to innovation.

Part III: The Truth About What You Say As a Leader

11. **Match Your Leadership Message to Your Audience**

    When it comes to communicating with others in the way that best suits other people, Markova, Dawna, *The Art of the Possible: A Compassionate Approach to Understanding the Way People Think, Learn and Communicate,* Conari Press, 1991, and *The Open Mind: Exploring the 6 Patterns of Intelligence,* Conari Press,

1996, show you how to identify your own ways of processing information, as well as those of others. Markova writes a great deal on education and parenting, but her ideas are highly relevant to business. Another strong approach to the different ways in which people think, learn, communicate, and work is provided by Sternberg, Robert J., *Thinking Styles*, Cambridge University Press, 1999. It aims to sensitize employers, among others, to the ways in which stylistic differences can affect the way in which an individual's ability is perceived.

12. Impactful Leaders Speak Simply

Much of the good advice on speaking with impact, and on constructing a clear, simple message, is contained in books on presentation and public speaking.

Ailes, Roger, *You Are the Message: Secrets of the Master Communicators*, Irwin Professional Pub, 1987, places emphasis on the strong first impressions made by what you say and how you say it. Leeds, Dorothy, *PowerSpeak: Engage, Inspire, and Stimulate Your Audience,* Career Press, 2003, is the best thing on the market on this front, showing how to engage and maintain an audience's attention. Useful practical guidance is also offered by Toogood, Granville, N., *The Articulate Executive: Learn to Look, Act, and Sound Like a Leader*, McGraw-Hill, 1995, looking at every aspect of how you verbally present yourself to others. "One Theme" is one of his five key messages.

13. **Sound Bites Need to Sizzle**

For step-by-step guidance on how to build a short, sharp, and succinct message on any theme, consult Frank, Milo O., *How to Get Your Point Across in 30 Seconds or Less*, Pocket, 1990, with its witty advice on how to deliver "substance in seconds." Weissman, Jerry, *Presenting to Win: The Art of Telling Your Story*, FT Prentice Hall, 2006, meanwhile, offers pointers on how to capture your audience and secure those "A-ha!" moments. A brand new book on the subject also looks promising: Gaulke, Sue, *101 Ways to Captivate a Business Audience*, AMACOM, 1996 specifically offers a "steak and sizzle" technique, with tips on how to energize your voice and draw in your audience.

14. **Your Tone of Voice Should Command Attention**

Acting coach Patsy Rodenburg is the international authority on voice-training. Her Rodenburg, Patsy, *The Actor Speaks: Voice and the Performer*, Palgrave Macmillan, 2002, with a preface by Dame Judy Dench, offers the reader a complete voice workshop, touching on every aspect of vocal performance. Targeted at a broader audience, including business people, is Rodenburg, Patsy, *The Right to Speak; Working with the Voice*, Routledge, 1993, which claims to enable the reader to meet any speaking challenge with total self-assurance. For further actionable advice, try Grant-Williams, Renee, *Voice Power: Using Your Voice to Captivate, Persuade, and Command Attention*, American Management Association, 2002. Physical exercises help you with everything from public speaking to voice-mail messages. Finally, an emerging classic in this genre is Crannell, Kenneth C., *Voice and Articulation*, Wadsworth Publishing, 1999, a good all-rounder with particularly useful advice on accent reduction.

15. **Names Matter to People, So Get Them Right**

Erving Goffman's fascinating study on the ways in which losing your name may affect your sense of identity can be found in his seminal text, Goffman, Ervin, *Asylums: Essays on the Social Situation of Mental Patients and Other Inmates*, Anchor, 1961, an analysis of life in the closed world of "total institutions." On the more practical front, developing your memory through simple exercises can help with the retention of details, such as names. Two helpful and engaging books are Lorayne, Harry and Lucas, Jerry, *The Memory Book: The Classic Guide to Improving Your Memory at Work, at School, and at Play*, Ballantine Books, 1996, and Higbee, Kenneth L., *Your Memory: How It Works and How to Improve It*, Marlowe and Company, 2001.

16. **"Coming Attractions" Get Others Tuned in to Your Message**

Although there is nothing currently in print that is really useful on the subject of priming frames, there is plenty of good advice available on effective workplace communication to help you think about delivering clear and empowering introductions to your leadership messages. Alessandra, Tony, *Communicating at Work*, Fireside, 1993, is a well-written and thorough primer, while

Clampitt, Philip G., *Communicating for Managerial Effectiveness*, Sage Publications, 2004, has particularly strong advice on the principles behind effectively communicating change, an area where communication breakdowns or problems of understanding are all too common.

Part IV: The Truth About Leadership Vision

17. What's the Big Idea? Bring Your Guiding Rules into Everyday Organizational Life

More information about the Atlanta Braves' approach can be found in an interview with the Braves' executive vice president and general manager since 1990, John Schuerholtz, that appeared in the *Wall Street Journal*: Adams, Russell, "The Culture of Winning: Atlanta Braves Have Secured 14 Straight Divisional Titles, and Team's GM Tells Why," *Wall Street Journal (U.S. edition)*, pp. B1-B5, October 5, 2005. The Journal is a great source of articles on leadership issues. Schuerholz has a book, *Built to Win*, coming out in 2006. For another approach to communicating a shared strategy to team members, I suggest Hrebeniak, Lawrence G., *Making Strategy Work: Leading Effective Execution and Change*, Wharton School Publishing, 2005, which focuses on the decisions, processes, and actions that make strategy really work. Kaplan, Robert S., and Norton, David P., *The Balanced Scorecard: Translating Strategy into Action*, Harvard Business School Press, 1996, offers a particular template—the "balanced scorecard" of the title—to help organizations move from ideas to action.

18. **Stories Help to Make Change Clear**

Allan, Julie, Fairtlough, Gerard, and Heinzen, Barbara, *The Power of the Tale: Using Narratives for Organisational Success*, John Wiley & Sons, 2002, is the best of many texts that have emerged in recent years on the applications of storytelling in business. It shows the role that shared stories can play in generating collective identity and values in today's companies, while providing general priming information on narrative and stories. This is complemented by Simmons, Annette, *The Story Factor: Inspiration, Influence, and Persuasion Through the Art of Storytelling*, Perseus Books Group, 2002, with its dozens of examples of effective storytelling in organizations worldwide and its deconstruction of the fundamental elements of a good story. You might also gain insight from Denning, Stephen, *The Leader's Guide to Storytelling: Mastering the Art and Discipline of Business Narrative*, Jossey-Bass, 2005, with its message that the best way to communicate with people is often a story.

19. **Playing Out the Tape Helps Others Prepare for the Future**

The writer and thinker who best articulates this subject, through his groundbreaking concept of "time horizons," is sociologist Elliot Jaques. A "time horizon" is the maximum time span a person can comfortably work with, and the longer one's time horizon, the greater one's capacity to lead and innovate. His classic on the concept is Jaques, Elliot, *Levels of Abstraction in Logic and Human Action*, Cason Hall & Co Pub, 1978. More pragmatic everyday approaches are offered by Larkin, Sandar and Larkin, T.J., *Communicating Change: Winning Employee Support for New Business Goals*, McGraw-Hill, 1994, which offers specific ideas for communicating messages about an organization's future right through the hierarchy, and Shaffer, Jim, *The Leadership Solution: Say It Do It*, McGraw-Hill, 2000, with its complete communication program to focus employees on both an organization's vision and the strategy required to get there.

20. Leaders Frame the Discussion

There is only one real expert to recommend here—the eminent linguist George Lakoff. His most well-known publication, Lakoff, George, *Don't Think of an Elephant: Know Your Values and Frame the Debate—The Essential Guide for Progressives*, Chelsea Green Publishing Company, 2004, presents a strong and clear argument for the careful choice of language to influence how people perceive an idea or an event, all through the example of recent politics. Lakoff, George and Johnson, Mark, *Metaphors We Live By*, University of Chicago Press, 2003, offers a different perspective on how your choice of language affects the way in which people respond to you.

Part V: The Truth About Leadership Presence and Power

21. A Leader is Always "On"

Given the parallels between the leader's role and that of the actors, it is no surprise that there are a number of books out there that present advice to business people from the actor's perspective. Halpern, Belle Linda and Lubar, Kathy, *Leadership Presence: Dramatic Techniques to Reach Out, Motivate, and Inspire*, Gotham Books, 2004, is the best of the bunch, offering a straightforward model and practical advice on how to develop stage, or leadership, presence. Also of value is Wydro, Kenneth, *Think on Your Feet: The Art of Thinking and Speaking Under Pressure*, Prentice Hall, 1981, with its holistic yet no-nonsense approach to generating presence, based around the idea of an "inner stillness" derived from relaxation and self-confidence.

22. Choose Your Battles Carefully

Whether we like it or not, any office is full of political wrangling. Luckily, there is plenty of good advice out there to help you keep your political capital accounts in the black. The best of the best include DuBrin, Andrew J., *Winning Office Politics: DuBrin's Guide for the 90s*, Prentice Hall Press, 1990, a very comprehensive introduction for the novice office politician, and Singer Dobson, Michael and Singer Dobson, Deborah, *Enlightened Office Politics*, American Management Association, 2001, which takes a principled and ethical

212

approach to the whole issue. Also useful is Craig Scott, Susan, *Fierce Conversations: Achieving Success at Work and in Life, One Conversation at a Time*, Viking Adult, 2002, with clear instructions on open, direct, and constructive conversations with work colleagues.

23. Your Stress Ripples Across the Organization

As the chapter illustrates, there are two sides to stress reduction: the psychological and the physical. On the former front, I should first mention Fritz Perls, who I cite in the chapter. A good introduction to his work, and the revolutionary principles of his Gestalt therapy—helping the patient develop awareness of, and coordination between, all parts of his or her personality—can be found in Perls, Frederick S., and Perls, Fritz, *The Gestalt Approach and Eye Witness to Therapy*, Science and Behavior Books, 1973. Also focusing directly on mind, rather than body, is Carlson, Richard, *Don't Sweat the Small Stuff at Work: Simple Ways to Minimize Stress and Conflict While Bringing Out the Best in Yourself and Others*, Hyperion, 1999, offering proven advice on how to modify your outlook and behavior to reduce the impact of stress at work. Supplement this with practical advice from the inspiring Zeer, Darrin, *Office Yoga: Simple Stretches for Busy People*, Chronicle Books, 2000, designed for the novice, and the more comprehensive textbook and "bible of stress-management" Seaward, Brian Luke, *Managing Stress: Principles and Strategies for Health and Well-Being*, Jones & Bartlett Publishers, 2004.

24. **Let Your Energy Be Like Fine Champagne—Not Too Bubbly or Flat**

    This can be a particular issue for women, which is some of the best advice on this score in books specifically targeted at female executives. However, the advice is relevant to everyone. I recommend the section on "How You Sound" in Frankel, Lois P., *Nice Girls Don't Get the Corner Office: 101 Unconscious Mistakes Women Make That Sabotage Their Careers*, Warner Business Books, 2004. Of more general appeal is Myers McGinty, Sarah, *Power Talk: Using Language to Build Authority and Influence*, Warner Business Books, 2002. Written by a linguistics expert, it guides the reader toward a public speaking style that is effective and engaging on both group and one-on-one encounters. A thought-provoking and useful take on the broader issue of how others perceive your energy at work is provided by Weisinger, Hendrie, *Emotional Intelligence at Work*, Jossey-Bass, 1997. The advice will help you become direct and commanding without slipping into aggression.

25. **You Need to "Read" Like a Leader in the Blink of an Eye**

    Best-selling author Malcolm Gladwell offers an entertaining study into the reasons why, and the ways in which, human beings make decisions about each other and life's events in a matter of seconds. Use Gladwell, Malcolm, *Blink: The Power of Thinking Without Thinking*, Little, Brown, 2005, as a salutary reminder of how quickly people's impressions of you can be sealed. For further advice on how to ensure that you make the best possible impression, I suggest Benton, D.A., *Executive Charisma: Six Steps to Mastering the Art of Leadership*, McGraw-Hill, 2003. Convinced by research that charisma is not something that we are born with but something we acquire, Benton offers a 6-step approach for learning how to think, act, and relate to others like an executive who means business.

26. **Good Leadership Is the Wise Use of Power**

It's well worth the effort to read Machiavelli for yourself, rather than rely on the interpretations of others. A fine translation of the Italian classic is Machiavelli, Niccolo, *The Prince*, Bantam Classics, 1984. Or try a wider selection of his writing accompanied by some fine analysis, edited by two professors: Machiavelli, Niccolo, *The Portable Machiavelli*, Penguin, 1979. An interesting, contemporary, and female-focused approach to the issue of power in the workplace is provided by Rubin, Harriet, *The Princessa: Machiavelli for Women*, Dell, 1998, which urges women to play the game by their own rules. Also centered around women, but an inspiring read for both sexes, and for anyone looking for a more people-focused approach to power is Coughlin, Lin, Wingard, Ellen and Hollihan, Keith, *Enlightened Power: How Women are Transforming the Practice of Leadership*, Jossey-Bass 2005, with 40 essays on the challenges of taking on the mantle of power while still working collaboratively and positively.

Part VI: The Truth About Getting Things Done

27. Often the Best Decision Is Empowering Someone Else to Decide

A pair of essay collections offering a diverse range of perspectives on decision-making provide a good source of ideas on this theme. Drucker, Peter Ferdinand, Hammons, John, Keeney, Ralph, Howard, Raiffa, Hayashi, Alden, M., *Harvard Business Review on Decision Making*, Harvard Business School Press, 2001, takes a good look at the theory of decision-making. Koch, Stephen, J., Kunreuther, Howard, C., Gunther, Robert, E. (eds), *Wharton on Making Decisions*, Wiley, 2001, show how to apply the latest approaches in decision-making. If you are interested in learning more about the theory of decision-making—how people in organizations actually make decisions—I would suggest March, James G., *Primer on Decision Making: How Decisions Happen*, Free Press, 1994. If you just want to get on and decide, then try Yates, J. Frank, *Decision Management: How to Assure Better Decisions in Your Company*, Jossey-Bass, 2003, which offers advice on how to generate strong decision-making processes within your organization.

28. Adjust Your Leadership Style to Fit the Employee

Situational leadership is about adapting your style to the situation or circumstances. Blanchard, Ken and Zigarmi, Patricia, *Leadership and the One Minute Manager: Increasing Effectiveness Through Situational Leadership*, William Morrow, 1999, offers advice on how to decide what management style is suitable for what individual, as well as how to work with people to determine their preferred style. Hersey, Paul, *The Situational Leader*, Warner Books, 1985, is also very helpful on the topic of assessing the competence and motivation of those you work with, and then adapting your approach accordingly. For a slightly different take on the issue—focusing on the leader as colleague and facilitator rather than visionary and ruler—I recommend Williams, Dean, *Real Leadership: Helping People and Organizations Face Their Toughest Challenges*, Berrett-Koehler Publishers, 2005. It stresses the need for the leader to put him or herself in the situation where work is taking place, helping people analyze the challenges rather than operating from a distance.

29. No Good Deed Goes Unpunished

It's written for women, but much of the advice in this book is spot-on for men as well, particularly those who aren't Alpha Male by nature! Frankel, Lois P., *Nice Girls Don't Get the Corner Office: 101 Unconscious Mistakes Women Make That Sabotage Their Careers*, Warner Business Books, 2004, provides plenty of short, sharp nuggets of advice on how to behave with others at work, showing how often being kind and caring to others at work can backfire. Firm but fair is better! A fuller exploration of that theme, along with a five-point program for developing a strong management style, is offered by Gardiner, Gareth, *Tough-Minded Management: A Guide for Managers Who Are Too Nice for Their Own Good*, Ballantine

Books, 1993. There are occasions when extra toughness is required, as when change is happening in the organization, or when colleagues challenge or resist your requests. Linsky, Martin and Heifetz, Ronald, R., *Leadership on the Line: Staying Alive Through the Dangers of Leading*, Harvard Business School Press, 2002, examines four forms of resistance, with advice on how to respond to them without destabilizing yourself or the organization.

30. The Structure Is Not the Organization, Just As the Map Is Not the Territory

Robert Fritz is the founder of "structural consulting" and an expert on "learning organizations." He focuses on developing organizational structures that will break down barriers and facilitate learning and development. Fritz, Robert, *The Path of Least Resistance for Managers: Designing Organizations to Succeed*, Berrett-Koehler Publishers, 1999, explains his key principles. I also recommend Morgan, Gareth, *Images of Organization*, SAGE Publications, 1996, a classic that has influenced management thinking worldwide for many years, offering a range of different ways to understand the way your organization works. Galbraith, Jay, R., *Designing Organizations: An Executive Guide to Strategy, Structure, and Process (Revised)*, Jossey-Bass, 2001, is another classic in the making. It discusses six main organization-shapers, exploring how organizational design, strategy, and structure should respond to these.

31. **Coming in from the Outside? Pay Your Dues!**

    Ciampa, Dan and Watkins, Michael, *Right From The Start: Taking Charge In a New Leadership Role*, Harvard Business School Press, 2005, contains advice as clear as its title! It's a survival guide for any leader entering a new organization. Conger, Jay A., *Winning Em Over: A New Model for Managing in the Age of Persuasion*, Simon & Schuster, 2001, focuses on one particular challenge you may face when you get there: resistance to new ideas and processes. Conger's book stresses teamwork as a leadership model, showing how constructive persuasion beats command-and-control when it comes to motivating people and getting them on board. As the chapter case-study shows, people resist less when they feel you are listening to their concerns and respecting their experience. Oakley, Ed, *Enlightened Leadership*, Fireside, 1994, explains why leaders who ask questions help themselves and the organization more than leaders who give answers.

32. **Delegation Is a Confidence Game**

    Landsberg, Max, *The Tao of Coaching: Boost Your Effectiveness at Work by Inspiring and Developing Those Around You*, Profile Books, 2003, has a good chapter on delegation and deals with such skills as motivating others and diagnosing their individual levels of skill and will. As most wise writers on this topic stress, employees will deal with delegated tasks better if they feel that others believe they can do them and trust them to get on with the job. Blanchard, Kenneth M., Carlos, John P., and Randolph, Alan, *Empowerment Takes More Than a Minute*, Berrett-Koehler Publishers, 2001, uses a fable to explore the concept of empowerment, showing how you can give your employees the authority and knowledge to act on their own within a shared structure of values and aims.

Part VII: The Truth About Motivating and Inspiring Your Team

33. Questions Unite; Answers Divide

I must credit Lucy Neal, co-founder of the groundbreaking London International Festival of Theatre, for the title of this chapter. As for advice on putting that concept into practice, I would once again recommend Oakley, Ed, *Enlightened Leadership*, Fireside, 1994. Oakley stresses that an enlightened leader asks effective questions to empower and energize their team, helping them to tackle obstacles and challenges with creativity and confidence. The theory behind such ideas is developed in Browne, M. Neil and Keeley, Stuart, M., *Asking the Right Questions: A Guide to Critical Thinking, Seventh Edition*, Prentice Hall, 2003, a classic on developing the skills to help yourself (and others) to engage with complex ideas and take a rational approach to resolving difficult challenges, by yourself or in the company of others. For more everyday, practical suggestions that can be applied immediately, try one of the books of "ready-made" questions that are available on the market. Two of the best are Finlayson,

Andrew, **Questions that Work**, American Management Association, 2001, and Leeds, Dorothy, **Smart Questions: The Essential Strategy for Successful Managers**, Berkley Trade, 2000.

34. Feedback Is the Best Kind of Criticism

Giving feedback well is one of the major challenges in the leadership world. You need to push people forward with your critique, but not criticize them so much that they feel overwhelmed or disheartened. Fulmer, Robert J., and Conger, Jay Alden, **Growing Your Company's Leaders: How Great Organizations Use Succession Management to Sustain Competitive Advantage**, American Management Association, 2003, covers the topic of leadership development in general, but has good advice on using stretch goals in feedback to stimulate the very best in people. Weisinger, Hendrie, **The Power of Positive Criticism**, American Management Association, 1999, focuses more directly on the topic of feedback, helping readers turn criticism into a powerful tool for organizational success, an approach shared by Rubin, Irwin M., Campbell, Thomas J., **The ABCs of Effective Feedback: A Guide for Caring Professionals**, Jossey-Bass, 1997. If you're interested in implementing a rigorous feedback system, Lepsinger, Richard and Lucia, Anntoinette D., **The Art and Science of 360 Degree Feedback**, Pfeiffer, 1997, offers case studies and a clear roadmap for introducing the effective 360° system into an organization, while Armstrong, Sharon and Appelbaum, Madelyn, **Stress-Free Performance Appraisals: Turn**

Your Most Painful Management Duty into a Powerful Motivational Tool, Career Press, 2003, performs a similar function for performance reviews.

35. **You Have More Than the Carrot and the Stick**

The study of high school students mentioned in the chapter comes from the following article: Janofsky, Michael, "Students Say High School Let Them Down," *The New York Times*, July 16, 2005. When it comes to adult employees, studies have shown that a primary reason people lose motivation at work is a lack of challenge or opportunities for growth. Byham, William C., Smith, Audrey B., and Paese, Matthew J., *Grow Your Own Leaders: How to Identify, Develop, and Retain Leadership Talent*, Financial Times Prentice Hall, 2002, stresses this point and proposes a targeted method for spotting, developing, and supporting talented individuals. A broader and more theoretical approach to the subject is offered by Thomas, Kenneth W., *Intrinsic Motivation at Work: Building Energy & Commitment*, Berrett-Koehler Publishers, 2002. Thomas stresses that passion for and fulfillment from work will always motivate people more than salaries, bonuses, and other extrinsic rewards. For a lighter touch, or a flash of inspiration, browse through Chandler, Steve and Richardson, Scott, *100 Ways To Motivate Others: How Great Leaders Can Produce Insane Results Without Driving People Crazy*, Career Press, 2004.

36. Quick Coaching Keeps Your Team on Course

The ideas in this chapter are influenced by the work of coach Michael Neill. Read more about his thinking at www.michaelneill.com. If you are keen to start doing some quick coaching yourself, there are a number of excellent guides on the market for people of all levels of experience. Hudson, Frederic M., *The Handbook of Coaching: A Comprehensive Resource Guide for Managers, Executives, Consultants, and HR*, Jossey-Bass, 1999, gives a thorough overview of coaching practice and the results that coaching can deliver. Whitmore, John, *Coaching for Performance: Growing People, Performance and Purpose*, Nicholas Brealey Publishing, 2002, is a classic in the field, with a model for coaching that involves carefully asking questions and listening well to the answers. Landsberg, Max, *The Tao of Coaching: Boost Your Effectiveness at Work by Inspiring and Developing Those Around You*, Profile Books, 2003, is also good.

37. Little Things Mean a Lot

Advice on the kind of details that will help you attract, motivate, and retain good staff can be found in Branham, F. Leigh, *Keeping the People Who Keep You in Business: 24 Ways to Hang on to Your Most Valuable Talent*, American Management Association, 2000, with its 24 Retention Practices. Shannon, Jane, *73 Ways to Improve Your Employee Communication Program*, Davis & Company, 2002, does a similar thing, but with the focus on what you say to staff and how you say it. Looking at the issue from the other side, you may want to avoid doing or saying those little things that can gradually push valuable employees away from an organization. Leigh Branham can help you with that, too, in Branham, Leigh, *The 7 Hidden Reasons Employees Leave: How to Recognize the Subtle Signs and Act Before It's Too Late*, American Management Association, 2005.

Part VIII: The Truth About Molding Your Team

38. A Leader Cares Passionately About Developing People

Bossidy, Larry, Charan, Ram, and Burck, Charles, *Execution: The Discipline of Getting Things Done*, Crown Business, 2002, with its focus on the development of a performance culture—a culture that rewards execution—is a development classic. Another well-thumbed text is Maslow, Abraham H., *Maslow on Management*, Wiley, 1998, with its brilliant analysis of how to develop a healthy, happy, and productive organization through strong leadership. Maslow wrote this many years ago, but the thinking is as relevant as ever. Two more recent publications that offer structured and actionable advice on improving your staff development are Bolt, James F., McGrath, Michael, and Dulworth, Mike, *Strategic Executive Development: The Five Essential Investments*, Pfeiffer, 2005, and Ulrich, David and Brockbank, Wayne, *The Hr Value Proposition*, Harvard Business School Press, 2005, with its practical tools and worksheets.

39. Succession Planning Ensures Your Bench Strength

A landmark book on this subject, although not an easy or quick read, is Rothwell, William J., *Effective Succession Planning: Ensuring Leadership Continuity and Building Talent from Within*, AMACOM, 2005. It offers strong methodology and rigorous guidelines for managing and filling organizational vacancies over the long term. Other recommended reads are Charan, Ram, Drotter, Stephen, and Noel, James, *The Leadership Pipeline: How to Build the Leadership Powered Company*, Jossey-Bass, 2000, with its advice on how to avoid knots and blockages forming in an organization's people development pipeline, and Berger, Lance A. and Berger, Dorothy R., *The Talent Management Handbook: Creating Organizational Excellence by Identifying, Developing, and Promoting Your Best People*, McGraw-Hill, 2003. The latter is full of straightforward and actionable advice for cultivating your best people.

40. Your Team Is Key to Your Success, So Vet Them Well

You can find the best advice on finding the best people in Smart, Bradford D., *Topgrading: How Leading Companies Win by Hiring, Coaching, and Keeping the Best People, (Revised and Updated Edition)*, Portfolio Hardcover, 2005, based on more than 4,000 interviews and case studies. Another set of guidelines to building a great team can be found in Collins, Jim, *Good to Great: Why Some Companies Make the Leap... and Others Don't*, Collins, 2001, based on the idea of getting the right people "on the bus." A vital element of crafting that great team is the quality of team communication. Comprehensive advice on that score can be found in Beverlein, Michael, Freedman, Sue, McGee, Craig, and Moran, Linda, *Beyond Teams: Building the Collaborative Organization*, Pfeiffer, 2002.

41. Dedicate Your Coaching Time Where It Does the Most Good

Morgan, Howard, Harkins, Phil, and Goldsmith, Marshall, *The Art and Practice of Leadership Coaching: 50 Top Executive Coaches Reveal Their Secrets*, John Wiley & Sons, 2004, offers just what it says on the cover: expert guidance on helping your team members to achieve their very best. Another interesting perspective on coaching people with a light yet focused touch is given by McKenna, Patrick J. and Maister, David H., *First Among Equals: How to Manage a Group of Professionals*, Free Press, 2002, with methods for building rapport and for working effectively with people of different ability, as well as for guiding people who resist being managed.

42. Awkward Discussions Are Tough: Play Offense, Not Defense

It's possible to achieve your objective from an awkward discussion without needlessly hurting the other person involved. So say the authors in Stone, Douglas, Patton, Bruce, and Heen, Sheila, *Difficult Conversations: How to Discuss What Matters Most*, Penguin Putnam, 2000, as they deconstruct those tricky encounters into their core components, helping readers prepare themselves in advance. Further techniques are provided in Patterson, Kerry, Grenny, Joseph, McMillan, Ron, Switzler, Al, and Covey, Stephen R., *Crucial Conversations: Tools for Talking When Stakes are High*, McGraw-Hill, 2002, applicable not only in business but in wider life.

Part IX: The Truth About Your Leadership Reputation

43. Ideas Come Across Differently with Different Media

One of the best books for writing for public or media consumption is Wilcox, Dennis L., *Public Relations Writing and Media Techniques*, Allyn & Bacon, 2004, with step-by-step guidance for producing effective written materials. It also covers writing for news media. When it comes to meeting the press, or going before the cameras, you need something like Stewart, Sally, *Media Training 101: A Guide to Meeting the Press*, Wiley, 2003. Written by a former reporter, it offers advice on how to determine your key message points in order to control the way your company comes across. Similarly practical advice is offered by Merlis, George, *How to Make the Most out of Every Media Appearance*, McGraw-Hill, 2003.

44. You Can't Hide the Sun with Your Hand: Be Honest

I recommend two different sets of reading here. The first texts address the subject of dealing effectively with external communications, particularly the press. Cohn, Robin, *The PR Crisis Bible: How to Take Charge of the Media When All Hell Breaks Loose*, Truman Talley Books, 2000, stresses the need to be well prepared for the possibility of a public relations crisis so that you can take control as soon as the emergency happens. Taylor, Ian, *Never Say "No Comment"*, L B Publishing Services, 2003, is a straight-talking guide to media relations. The second group looks at engendering a culture of honesty within the organization. Gaffney, Steven, *Honesty Works! Real-World Solutions to Common Problems at Work & Home*, JMG Publishing, 2005, is a practical, easy read, accompanied by exercises, which encourages readers to confront tricky situations head-on. More focused on working life is Johnson, Larry and Phillips, Bob, *Absolute Honesty: Building a Corporate Culture That Values Straight Talk and Rewards Integrity*, AMACOM, 2003, offering an action plan for building an environment of absolute honesty.

45. **Spouses and Partners Must Be on Their Best Behavior**

The information on guidance for wives featured in this chapter was sourced from the article "Breaking Out: the Wives Who Say No," *The London Sunday Times, News Review*, June 17 1999, p.1. Perhaps not surprisingly, there really are not any good books out there on how spouses should behave in this day and age. However, if you and your spouse are keen to find out more, it does no harm to "gen up" on the subject of etiquette so that you are at home in any work or social situation. The classic in this field is by Emily Post, now brought up-to-date by a relative: Post, Peggy, *Emily Post's Etiquette (16th Edition)*, Collins, 1997, covers the subject of good manners with a contemporary slant, with new sections on cell phone and email behavior! Male spouses may enjoy Bridges, John, *How to Be a Gentleman: A Contemporary Guide to Common Courtesy*, Rutledge Hill Press, 2001. Nor does it do any harm to hone your skills of social communication. Carducci, Bernardo J., *The Pocket Guide to Making Successful Small Talk: How to Talk to Anyone Anytime Anywhere About Anything*, Pocket Guide Company, 1999, explains what small talk is all about, how to prepare yourself for it, and the physical and mental barriers that can get in your way.

46. You Don't Get Your Meat Where You Get Your Potatoes

Not much gets written about sexual politics in the workplace, and to a certain extent, further reading is not required—the point is a simple one: don't do it! However, in the contemporary working climate, it may prove edifying, even interesting, to learn more about the subject of sexual harassment: what constitutes it and how to deal with it. Of the two books I recommend, one takes a very practical perspective: Boland, Mary L., *Sexual Harassment in the Workplace*, Sphinx Publishing, 2005, explores the issues and occurrences that can lead to complaints. The other analyzes the whole idea of sexual harassment and how it is interpreted by different cultures. Cope Saguy, Abigail, *What Is Sexual Harassment?: From Capitol Hill to the Sorbonne*, University of California Press, 2003, explores the ways in which sexuality is used to gain power in the workplace.

47. **Don't Get Tangled in the Grapevine**

Some of the best advice for keeping yourself clear of the tangles of office gossip can be found in books on office politics. See those that I recommend in the notes for Truth 22. For another perspective on this issue, exploring the ways in which knowledge informally spreads through an organization, for the good as well as the bad, take a look at the fascinating Cross, Robert and Parker, Andrew, *The Hidden Power of Social Networks: Understanding How Work Really Gets Done in Organizations*, Harvard Business School Press, 2004. This is a comprehensive work on the way in which social networks function between co-workers.

Part X: The Truth About Your Connections

48. **You Can't Microwave Your Leadership Relationships**

Solomon, Robert C. and Flores, Fernando, *Building Trust: In Business, Politics, Relationships, and Life*, Oxford University Press, 2003, stresses trust as the foundation upon which all good relationships are built. This fascinating book offers perspectives on how one can develop authentic trust, through honesty and dialogue, with work colleagues. Guides to networking also offer plenty of advice relevant to the processes of building new working relationships. Two interesting ones are Bjorseth, Lillian D., *Breakthrough Networking: Building Relationships That Last, Second Edition*, Duoforce Enterprises, 2003, and Rezac, Darcy, Thomson, Judy, and

Hallgren-Rezac, Gayle, ***Work the Pond! Use the Power of Positive Networking to Leap Forward in Work and Life***, Prentice Hall Press, 2005.

49. **Your Network Is Your Lifeline to Influence and Information**

A network is something that needs constant attention. Relationships require careful maintenance. This message is stressed in Mackay, Harvey, ***Dig Your Well Before You're Thirsty: The Only Networking Book You'll Ever Need***, Currency, 1999, as the author shows you how to build a personal network that works for you. Baber, Anne and Waymon, Lynne, ***Make Your Contacts Count: Networking Know-How for Cash, Clients, and Career Success***, American Management Association, 2001, offers a similar take on the issue, presenting itself as a recipe book for networking, with practical strategic advice on how to up your visibility and your impact through connections with others. Frishman, Rick, Lublin, Jill, and Steisel, Mark, ***Networking Magic: Find the Best—from Doctors, Lawyers, and Accountants to Homes, Schools, and Jobs***, Adams Media Corporation, 2004, has a slightly different take on the issue, explaining how to find the best person in any field to help you with a particular issue or question.

50. **Peers and Power Are a Potent Mix**

Silberman, Melvin A., ***PeopleSmart***, John Wiley & Sons, 2005, is a book about building better relationships with people through becoming smarter about who they are and the way they work—a vital skill to apply with co-workers.

But what about those peers who are really out to cause you trouble? Look to Bramson, Robert M., *Coping with Difficult People: The Proven-Effective Battle Plan That Has Helped Millions Deal with the Troublemakers in Their Lives at Home and at Work*, Dell, 1988, for help, with its six basic steps for coping with anyone. In addition, Lencioni, Patrick M., *Silos, Politics, and Turf Wars: A Leadership Fable About Destroying the Barriers That Turn Colleagues Into Competitors*, Jossey-Bass, 2006, takes a creative approach to the issue, addressing the theme of interpersonal and inter-departmental conflict through an engaging story. And if you want to laugh about it, while getting some strong guidance on how to deal with the problem, I suggest Bernstein, Albert J. and Craft Rozen, Sydney, *Neanderthals at Work: How People and Politics Can Drive You Crazy...and What You Can Do About Them*, John Wiley & Sons Inc, 1992. It presents the unspoken rules of corporate life through characters you will recognize.

51. It's Lonely at the Top: Keep It That Way

There is only one book to mention here. Joni, Saj-Nicole, *The Third Opinion: How Successful Leaders Use Outside Insight to Create Superior Results*, Portfolio Hardcover, 2004, offer a unique perspective on how to find "thinking partners" outside your immediate leadership circle, with whom you can talk frankly and explore important issues, without damaging your leadership position.

52. Trust and Loyalty Are Long-Term Goals

Ciampa, Dan and Watkins, Michael, *Right from the Start: Taking Charge in a New Leadership Role*, Harvard Business School Press, 1999, is a core text on the subject of how you develop true and trusting relationships with work colleagues and staff, while Joni, Saj-Nicole, *The Third Opinion: How Successful Leaders Use Outside Insight to Create Superior Results*, Portfolio Hardcover, 2004, looks at issues of structural trust and how organizational design works against it. It is one of the few books that looks at whom to trust. Sally Bibb and Jeremy Kourdi, *Trust Matters: For Organisational and Personal Success*, Palgrave Macmillan, 2004, offers a good summary of the role of trust, and how to build it, in business relationships.

The Truth About Managing Your Career
...and Nothing But the Truth

BY KAREN OTAZO

This is your concise, fast-paced guide to achieving maximum career success. Drawing on her work with 2,000+ leaders and business professionals, and her analysis of hundreds of secret feedback reports, Dr. Otazo identifies 60 crucial career challenges—and winning solutions! Here are breakthrough techniques for succeeding at a new job...working more smoothly with bosses and colleagues...building a high performance personal network...managing your workload...deciding who to trust (and distrust)...handling enemies and overcoming setbacks... recognizing when to move on...getting noticed, getting ahead, getting to the top!

ISBN 0131873369, © 2006, 272 pp., $18.99

The Truth About Getting Your Point Across
...and Nothing But the Truth

BY LONNIE PACELLI

The Truth About Getting Your Point Across will help you communicate more powerfully in any situation: with executives, peers, subordinates, customers, partners, investors, or anyone else. Lonnie Pacelli presents world-class tips and techniques for every communication scenario: meetings, interviews, presentations, team leadership, brainstorming sessions, even elevator pitches. Need to gain credibility with your CEO? Provide better feedback? Motivate teams more effectively? Solve problems more rapidly? Whatever your communication challenge, this book offers proven, fast-access solutions!

ISBN 0131873717, © 2006, 272 pp., $18.99